Introduction

Welcome to a journey through time, a captivating photographic tour magazine that transcends the boundaries of the present and transports you to an era long gone by. In the pages that follow, you will embark on a remarkable adventure, one that allows you to traverse the annals of history with breathtaking photographs as your guide.

This magazine is a testament to the extraordinary preservation of a mining town's charm and character that has withstood the test of time. Step back in time as you witness the old-time boardwalks, the nostalgia-inducing ice cream parlor and soda fountain, the rustic western cafe, and the inviting mercantile store - all from a bygone era.

In these pages, you will find not just photographs but a portal to the past, a time machine of memories that evokes the sights, sounds, and flavors of yesteryears. The scenes captured in these images are not just frozen moments but living, breathing windows into the history of a town that once thrived with ambition and life.

The meticulous preservation of these historic treasures will kindle a sense of wonder and nostalgia within you. Every image tells a story, every storefront whispers secrets of times gone by, and every frame is a canvas of cherished memories waiting to be discovered.

Join us on this extraordinary journey, a voyage of nostalgia and exploration. As you turn the pages of this magazine, you will be transported through time, and you may even discover long-lost memories of your own. Welcome to an adventure where the past meets the present and where the art of photography allows us to share with you the history of this amazing place.

Written and photographed by Teresa & Keith Peters

Robson's Arizona Mining World

Robson's Arizona Mining World is one of the most interesting off-the-beaten-path locations that you will find in the desert. The best way to describe this place is to imagine if a mining museum and ghost town had a child, this would be it.

Robson's Arizona Mining World is located at 34° 1.296′ N, 113° 7.657′ W. in Aguila, Arizona, in Maricopa County, at the edge of one of the largest Saguaro forests in Arizona.

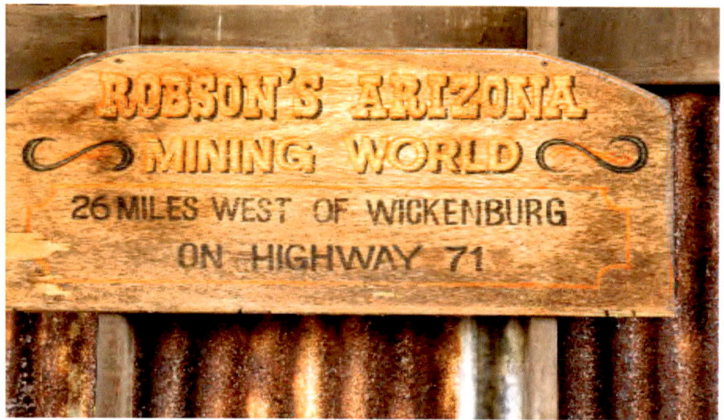

Getting There:

From Phoenix:
Take US Rt 60 Northwest to Wickenburg (54 miles); continue on through Wickenburg on US Rt 60 West toward Aguila (20 miles); turn right on AZ Rt 71 and go 4.1 miles to Robson's large sign on the left. Turn left.

From Las Vegas:
Take US Rt 93 South to Kingman, continue through Kingman on US Rt 93 Southeast to AZ Rt 71, and go right 11 miles to the large Robson sign on the right. Turn right.

From Southern California:
Take I 10 East through Blythe, CA, into Arizona (31 miles) and turn left Northwest on US RT 60 about 60 miles just past the little town of Aguila to AZ Rt 71 and turn left 4 1/2 miles to Robson's large sign on the left. Turn left.

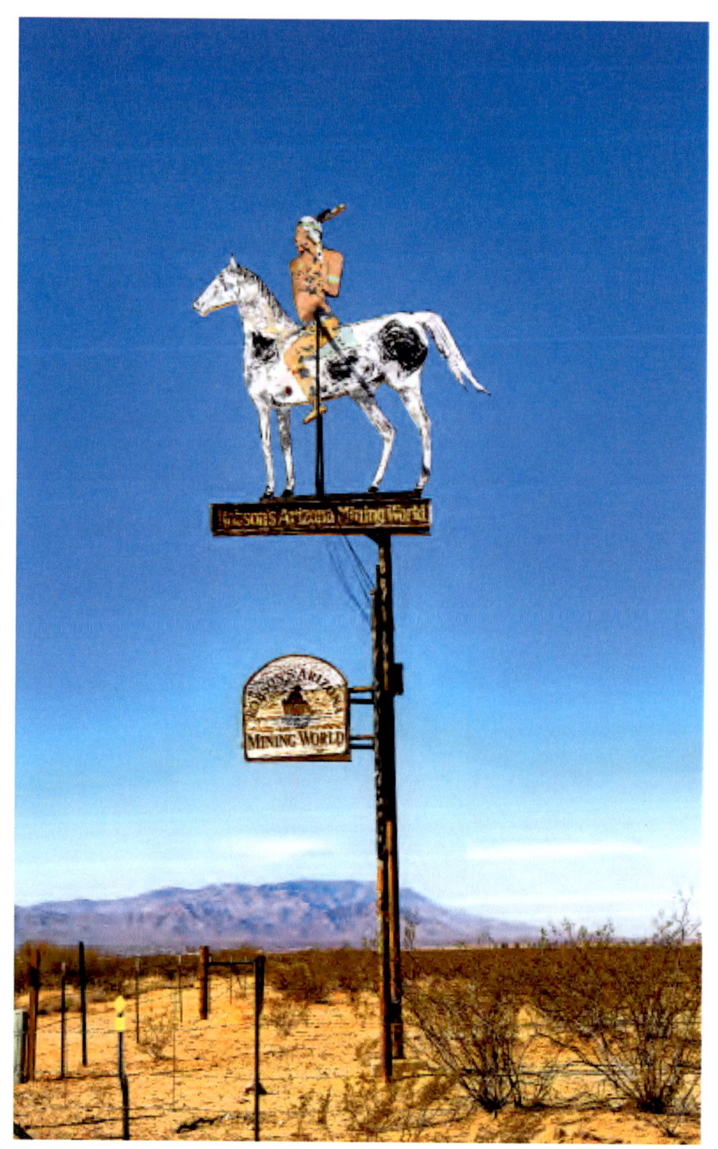

Arizona Mining History

We cannot talk about Robson's Arizona Mining World without talking about Arizona's mining history. The earliest miners in what is now Arizona were Native Americans who chiefly mined surface outcrops of salt, clays, hematite, quartz, obsidian, stone, turquoise, and coal. In the late 1600s, Spanish explorers hunted for metallic deposits with a special interest in gold and silver.

Antonio de Espejo made the first significant silver discovery south of the San Francisco Peaks in May 1583, near present-day Jerome, Arizona. By the late 17th Century, Spanish prospectors had engaged in extensive mining in the mountains bordering the Santa Cruz River and its tributary Sonoita Creek. Rare discoveries of sheets or "planchas" of silver – one sheet reportedly weighed 2700 pounds – fired the imaginations of several generations of miners.

In 1854, in Ajo, Arizona, the Arizona Mining and Trading Company launched the modern era of hard-rock mining. A burgeoning mining industry stimulated early growth in the Arizona Territory. And by 1864, nearly 25 percent of the male, non-native populace were prospectors.

By the 1870s, many hard rock mines were yielding prodigious volumes of copper, lead, zinc, silver, and gold ore. In 1912, the newly christened state of Arizona supported 445 active mines, 72 concentrating facilities, and 11 smelters with a gross value of nearly 67 million dollars -- equivalent to 1.4 billion dollars in 2006 dollars. (source Arizona Geological Survey)

Early Town History

In 1862-63, the Peeple Party discovered gold at Rich Hill, only 25 miles from the current location of what would become Robson's Mining World.
This find motivated the Westley Rush Family, who operated a large ranch out of Aguila, Arizona, to file a mining claim. In 1917 they opened the Gold Leaf Mine. The Westley Rush Family operated the mine until 1924 when Ned Creighton acquired the mine. Ned renamed the mine the Nella-Meda mine in honor of the two Rush Family daughters. At the height of the mining operation, the main shaft reached the 500ft level producing gold from .002 to 0.755 ounces of gold per ton.

In 1942 due to World War II, the federal government ordered all US gold mines shuttered. With the closure of the mine, the mining engineer, Harold Mason, was installed as the caretaker. Harold remained at the mine and eventually received the deed to the property.

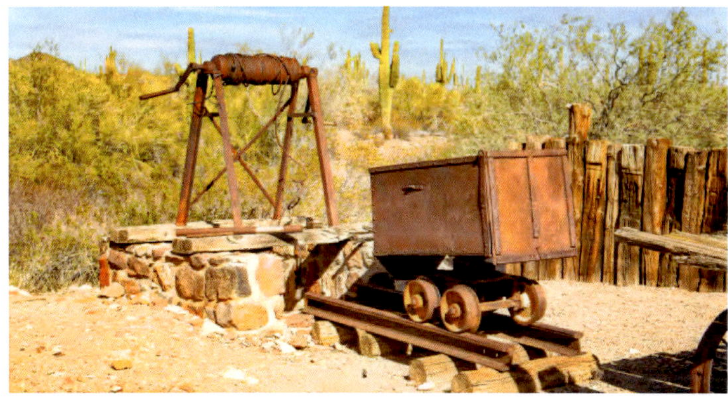

Hand Winch and Ore Car
During the early days of mining, hand winches were used to haul ore buckets out of the mine shafts.

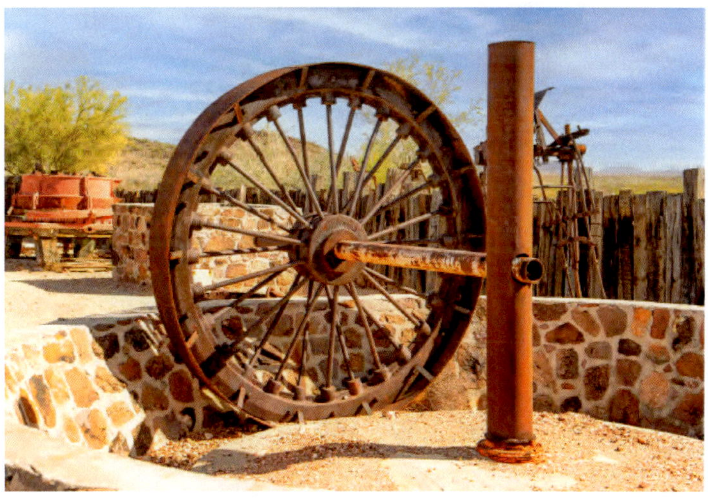

Chilean Arrastra
The arrastra was a common device used in the early days of mining, especially in the American West. It was a simple and effective way to crush and grind ore, and two large horses pulled the wheel in a circle to crush and grind the ore.

Charles was a man with a dream.

Charles Herbert Robson was born on March 23, 1931, in Pheonix. Charles was one of the largest beekeepers and hive product manu-facturers in Arizona. Charles was a renowned lecturer on the Nutritional and Medical uses of Hive products. In 1988, Charles wrote and published a book entitled Seven Health Secrets From the Hive, which sold worldwide and is currently available on Amazon.

Charles grew up with an acute interest in the history of early Arizona settlers. He loved to share his stories of Arizona History and, as a result, spent his life collecting anything related to "Old Arizona." As Charles' collection grew, he needed a place to store and display his col-lection. Charles was blessed that his wife, Jeri, shared his passion for Arizona's mining history.

Robson's Arizona Mining World is Born

To bring his dream to life, Charles purchased the Nella-Meda mine from Harlod in 1979.

In the late 1980s, Charles and Jeri embarked on their grand plan to bring the old mining camp back to life. They restored fourteen of the original buildings, moved buildings from other locations, and built new structures, in-cluding a 26-unit hotel and a fully functioning restaurant. They held their grand opening on January 19, 1992, showcasing 26 buildings filled with antiques and the most extensive col-lection of mining equipment anywhere.

From 1992 Charles and Jeri continued to oper-ate and expand their collection until Charles's death in 2009.

After Charles's death, Jeri turned the opera-tion of the property to Western Destinations in 2009 and used the location to hold corporate events until 2012, when disaster struck.

The hotel burned down, and the restaurant closed; this resulted in the town becoming

mostly deserted. In 2015 a caretaker was hired to maintain the property and provide guided tours to the public.

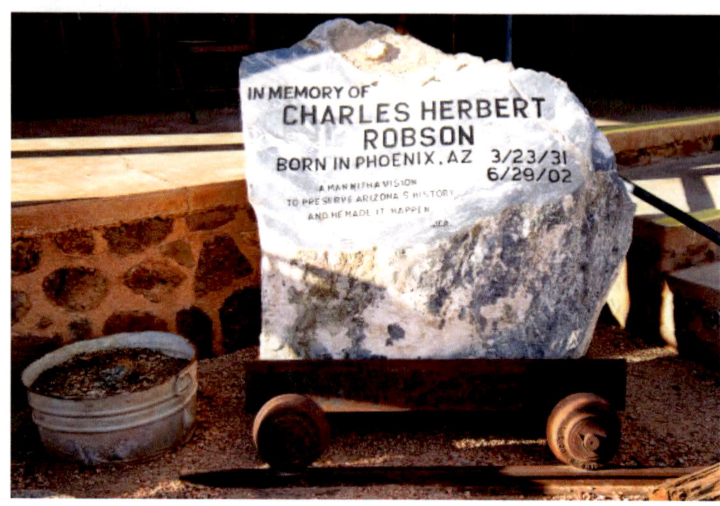

Charles Robson Memorial Stone
This memorial stone is located next the entry steps of the Livery Stable.

Welcome!

As you turn off Hwy 71 at the Robson's sign, you head west into the Sonoran Desert along a private road. After a mile and a half, the town appears.

Two halves of a massive flywheel frame the entrance. Once you pass these, you are transported back in time. The Liberty Stable and Nella-Meda Opera House are the first two buildings of the town.

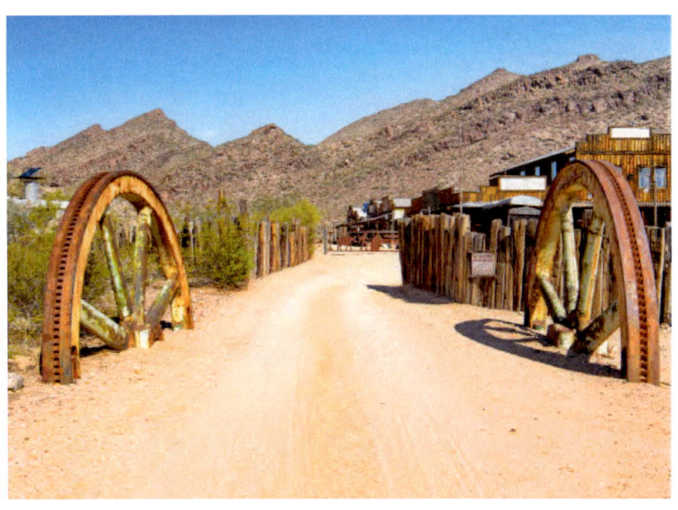

Huge Fly Wheel Halves
The huge flywheel halves framing the town's entrance were once bolted together to form a large flywheel used to ensure uniform mining equipment operations at the Live Oak Mine in Globe, Arizona.

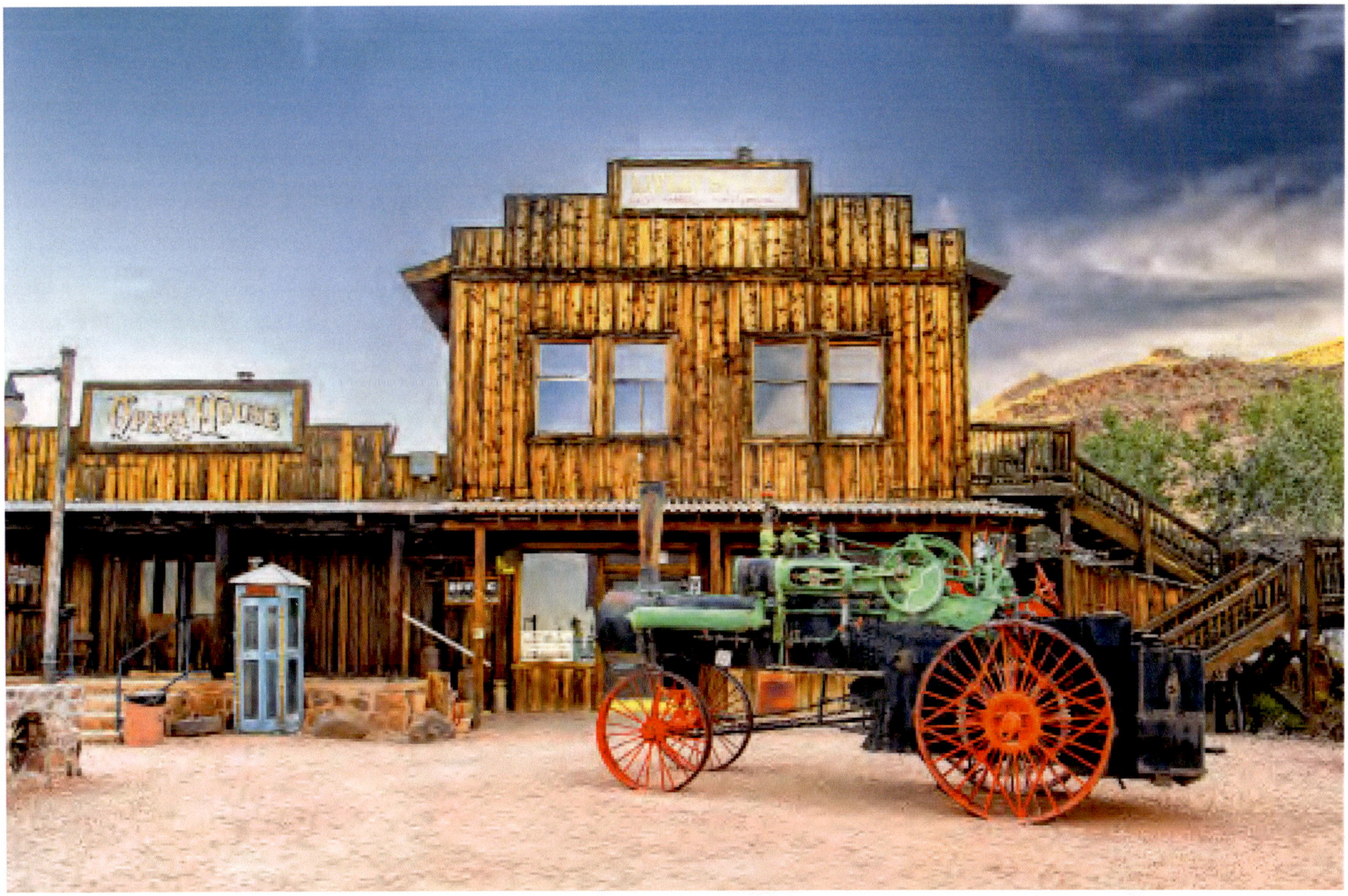

1910 J. I. Case Threshing Machine Traction Engine

Livery Stable- First Floor

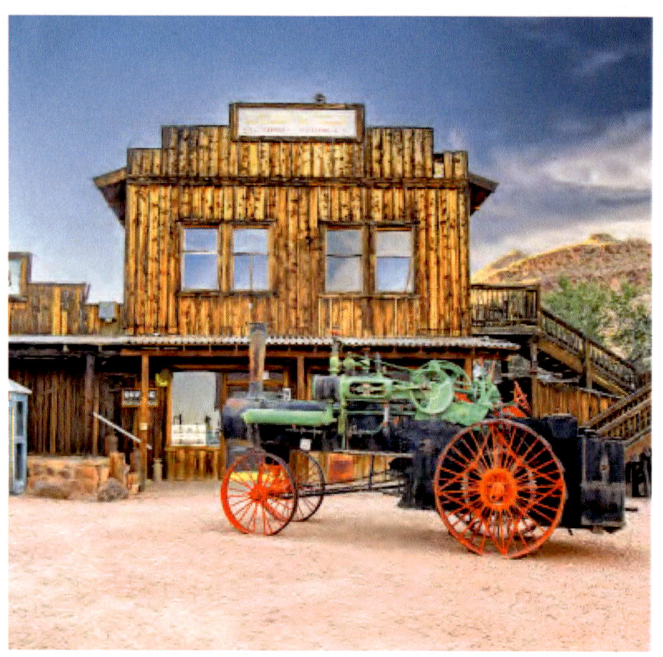

The Livery Stable is a two-story building custom-built to appear old to match the original buildings.

The street-level section is an old-time ice cream parlor.

In their heyday of the 1920s through the 1950s, ice cream parlors were popular gathering places for people of all ages. They were often social hubs where people could enjoy a sweet treat and spend time with friends and family.

Many ice cream parlors had a soda fountain like this one where patrons could order ice cream sodas, floats, and other classic fountain drinks. Some ice cream parlors also had a jukebox, which added to the lively atmosphere; this one includes a Rogola Player Piano to provide music for the patrons.

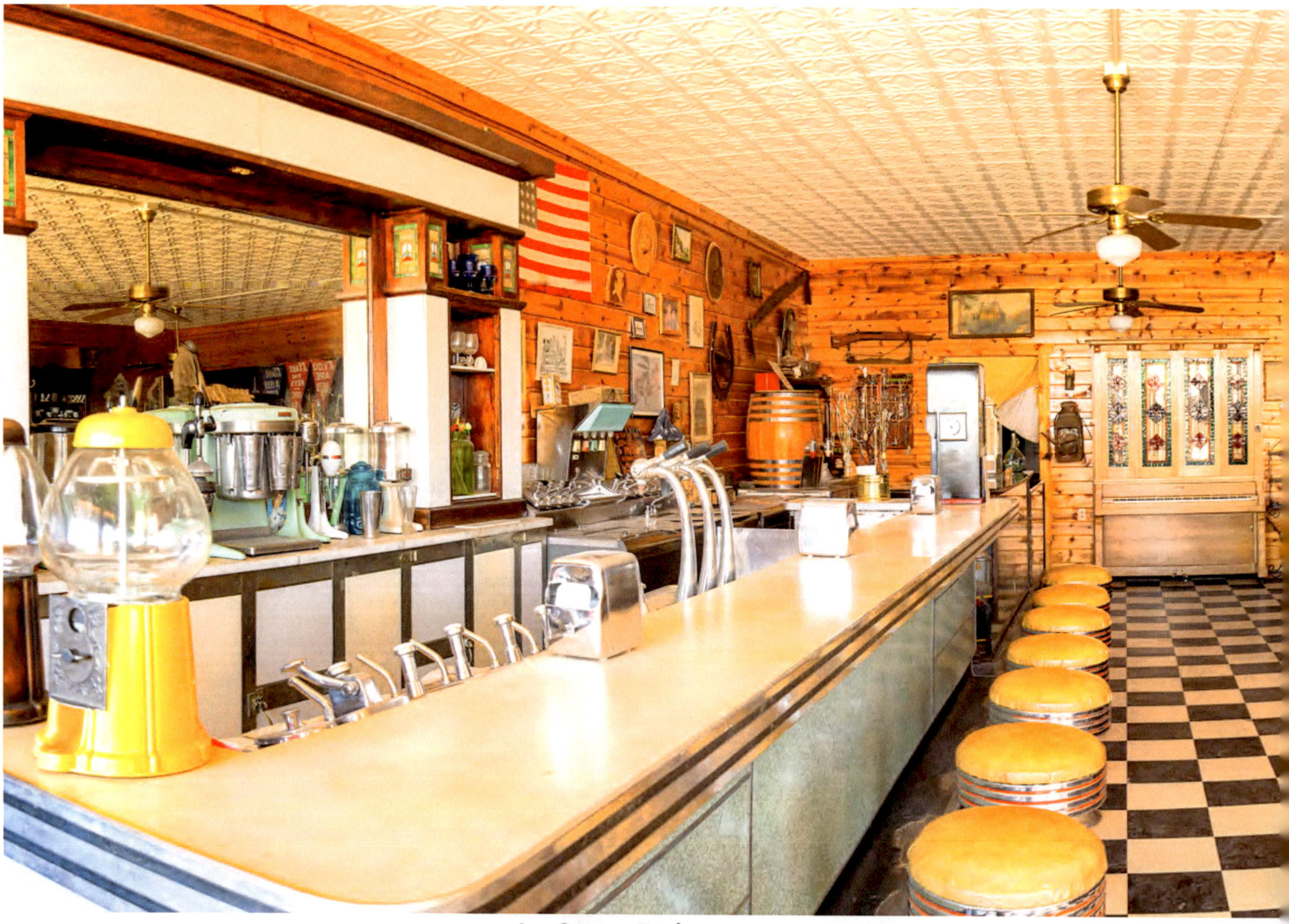

Ice Cream Parlor

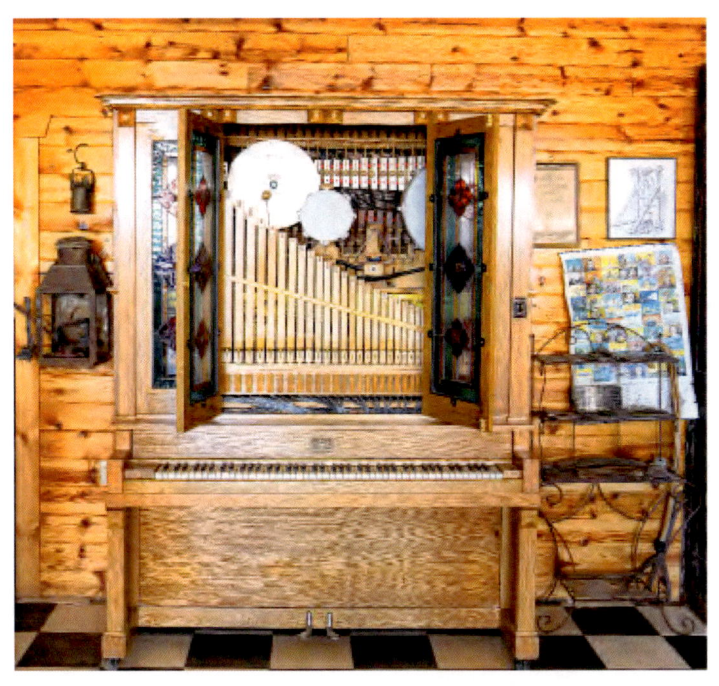

Rogola Player Piano

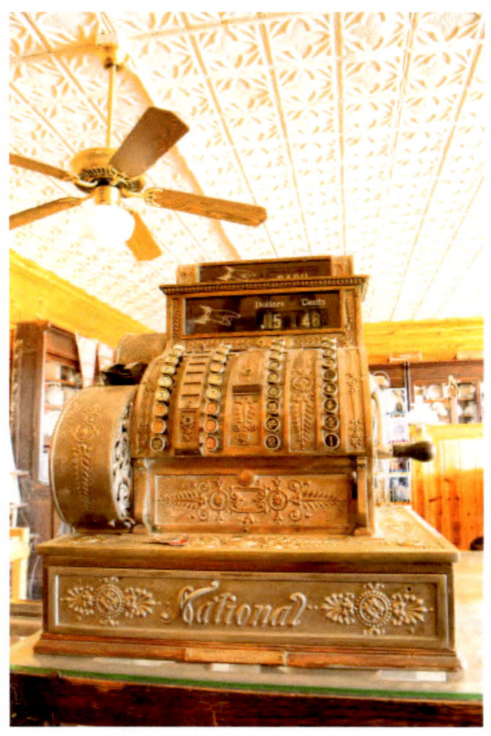

Vintage National Cash Register

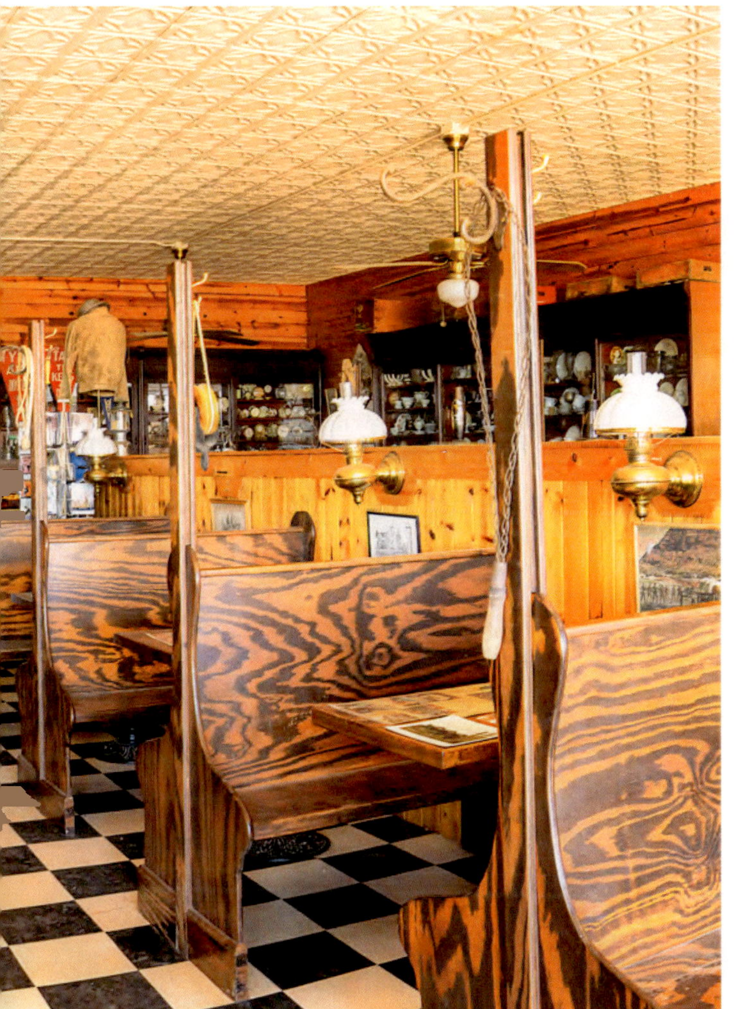

Charles purchased this ice cream parlor from Aguilar, Colorado, dismantled it, and transported and reassembled it here. And just like all of the other buildings, it is full of unique items.

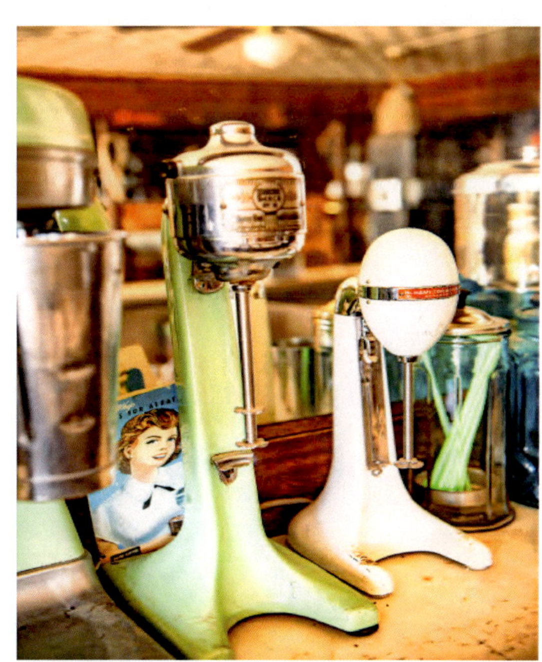

**Classic Hamilton Beach
Drinkmaster #51**

Livery Stable - Second Floor

The Second Floor was designed to support training, meetings, and other gatherings. It now houses a wide array of antiques of all kinds.

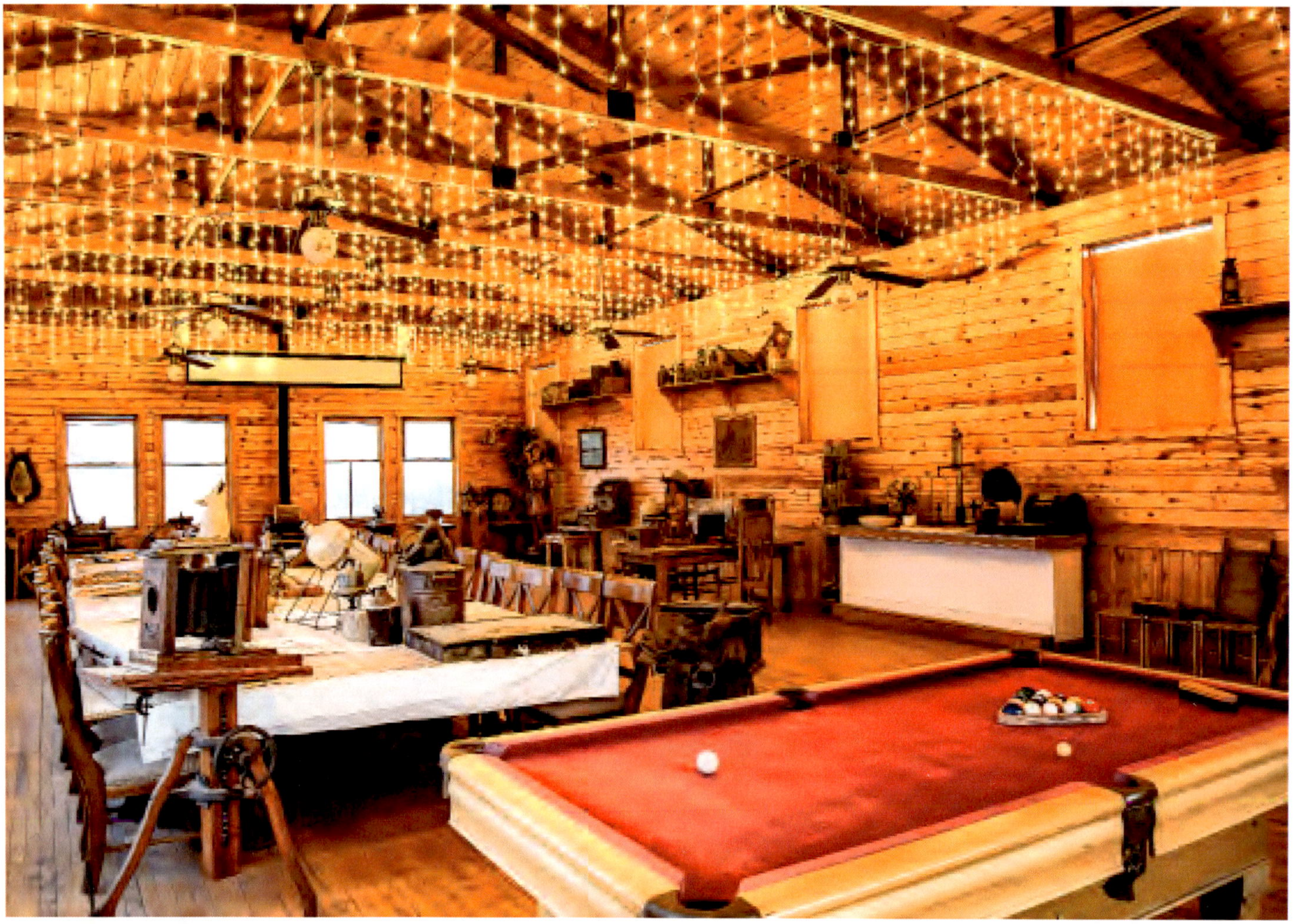

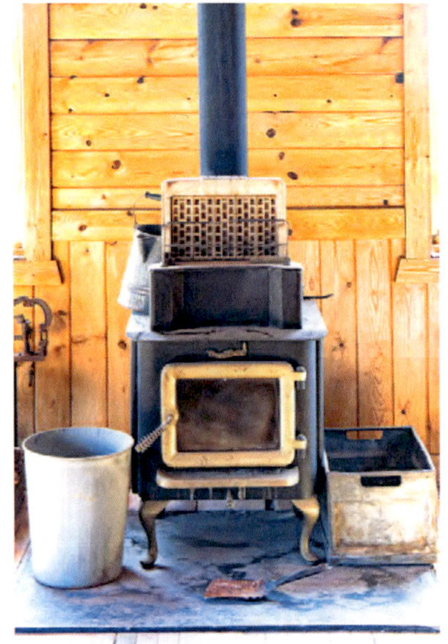

Coal Stove

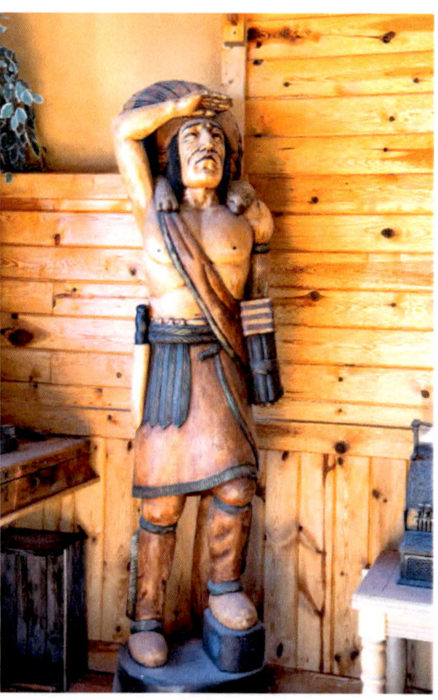

Cigar Store Indian

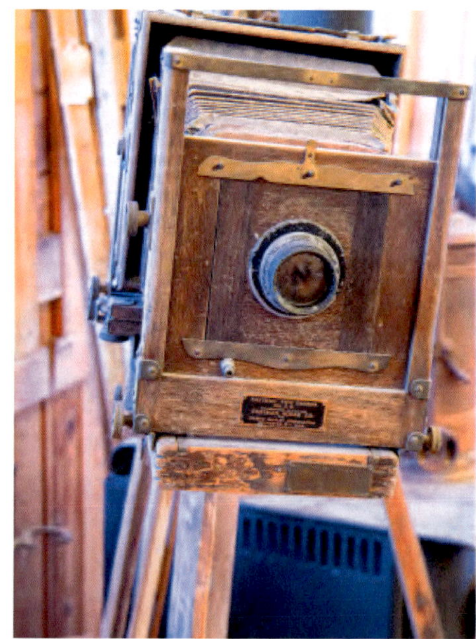

Eastman Kodak 2D Camera

Nella-Meda Opera House

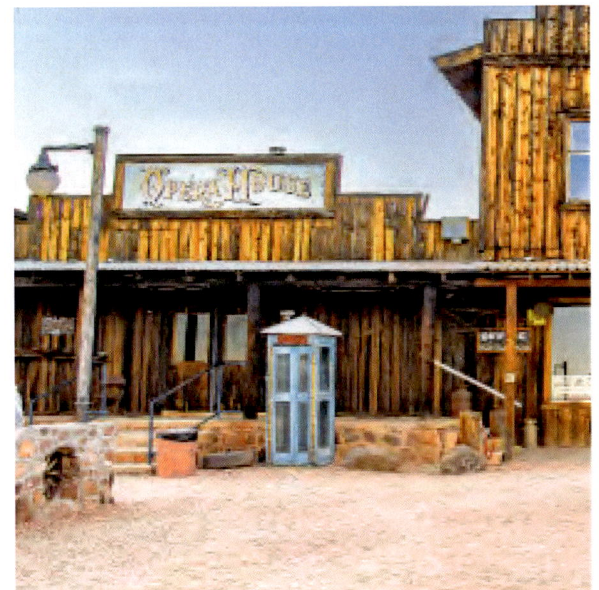

Nella-Meda Opera House has a stage and a large seating area. Along one wall is a massive display of mineral specimens; the opposite wall is the home to an extensive book collection.

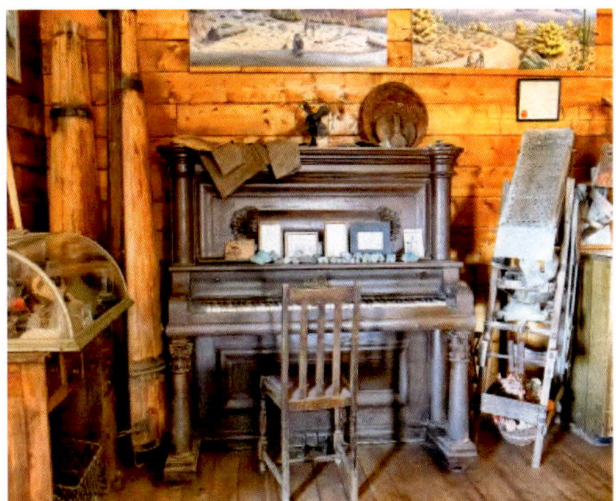

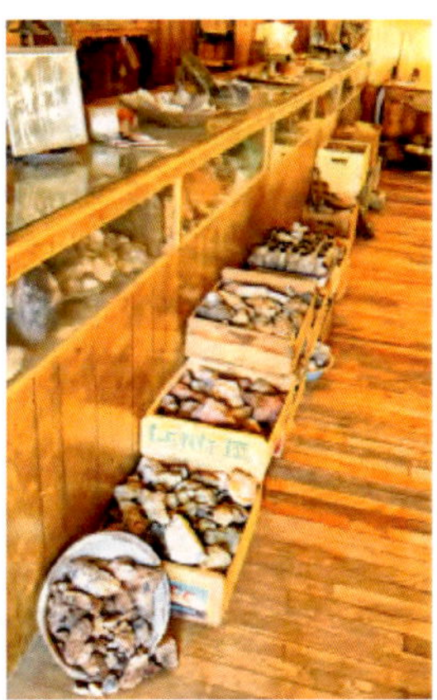

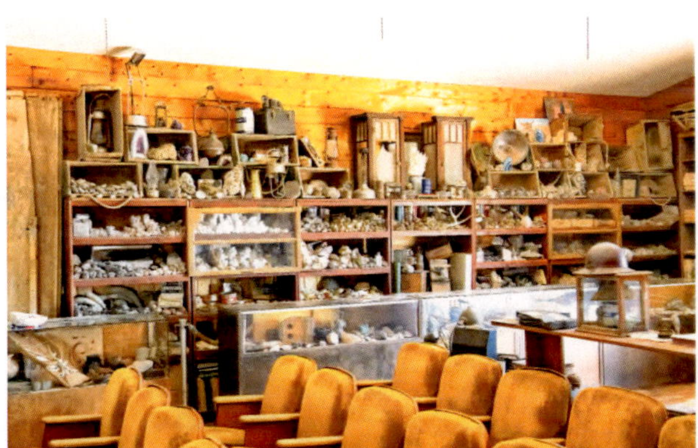

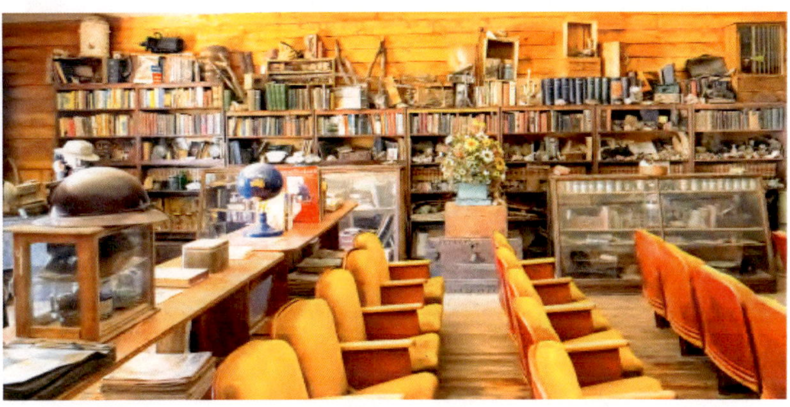

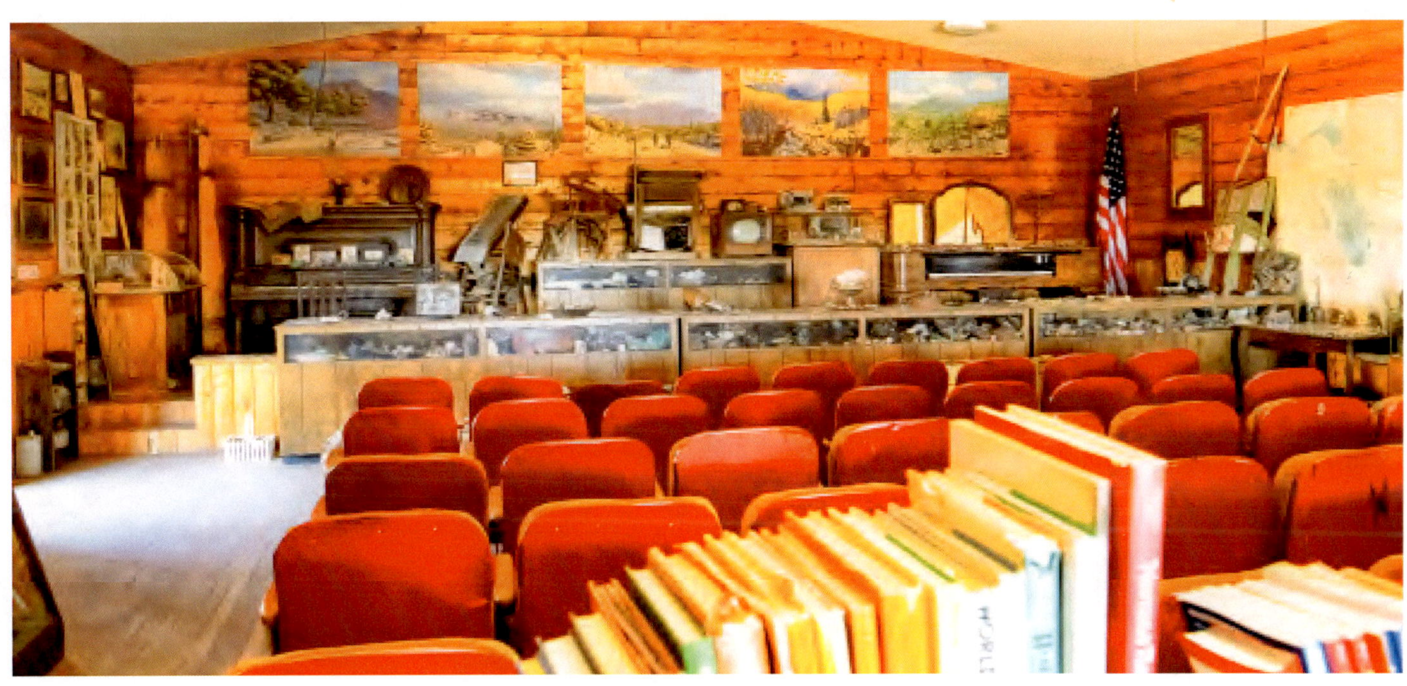

Opera House Interior

Main Street

Strolling along the wooden sidewalk, you are transported back in time to experience life in an early 20th-century mining town.
The North side of Main Street consists of five distinct *shops:*

- Gold Leaf Cafe
- The Mercantile
- Barbershop
- Assay Office
- Hillside Press
- The Generating Plant

Across the street you will find the largest collection of mining equipment in the U.S.

Beyond these buildings, you will find:

- The Blacksmith Shop
- The Machine Shop
- Firehouse
- Miners Cabins
- Chapel

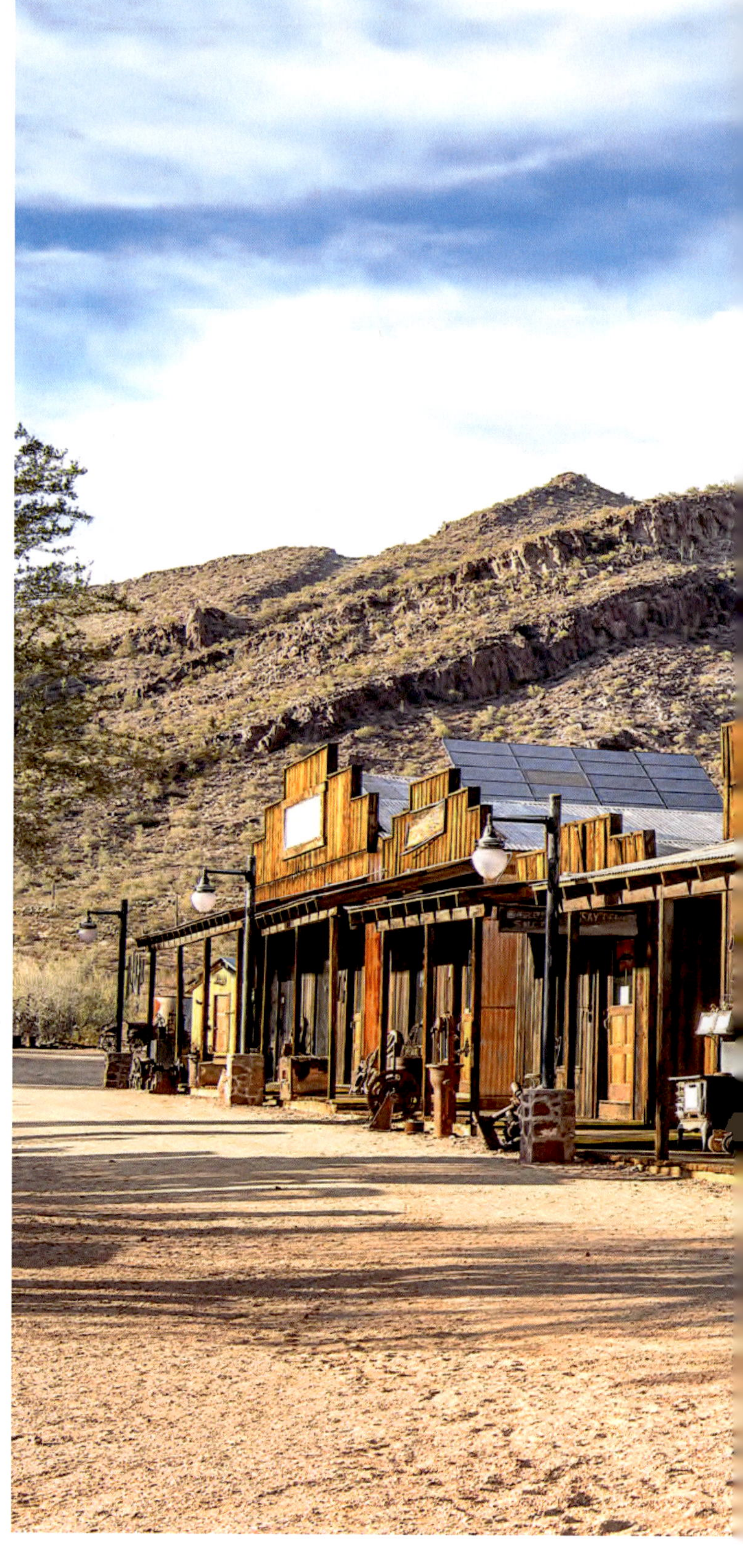

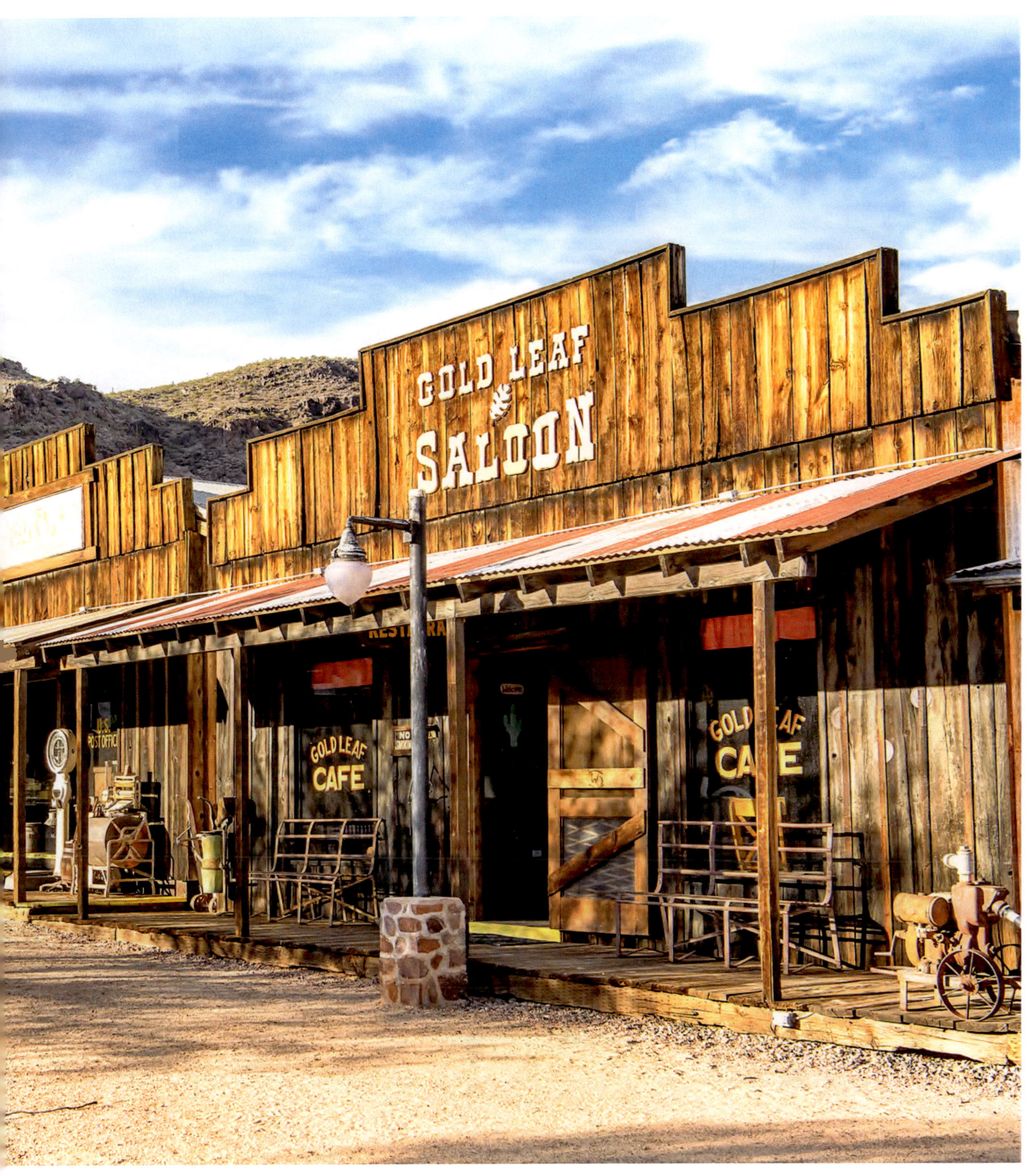

The Gold Leaf Cafe

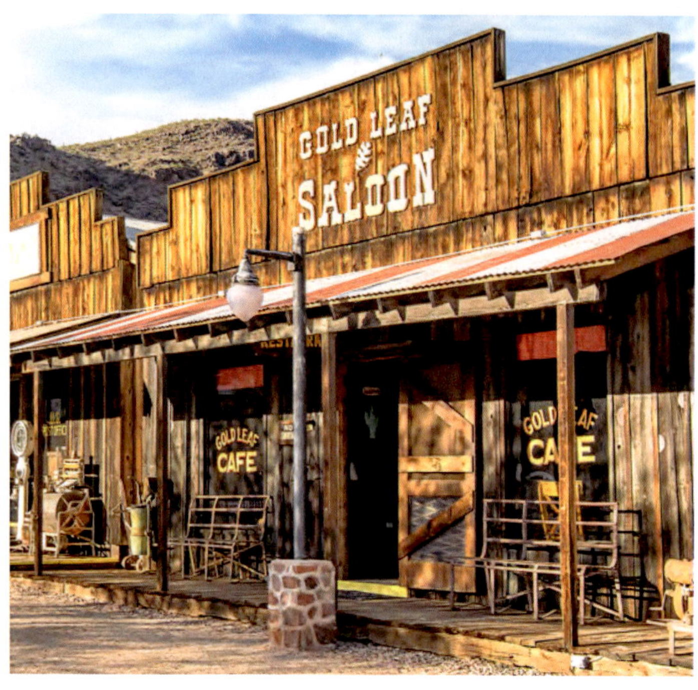

The Gold Leaf Cafe is the design of an early 1900s restaurant, complete with hardwood floors, an old heater in the back corner, and a collection of rifles on the walls.

Stepping inside the cafe, you have the feeling that you have been lucky to beat the lunch rush as each table is dressed with red and white checkered tablecloths and napkin holders.

You would never suspect that a fully functional modern commercial kitchen is behind the period swinging door at the cafe's rear.

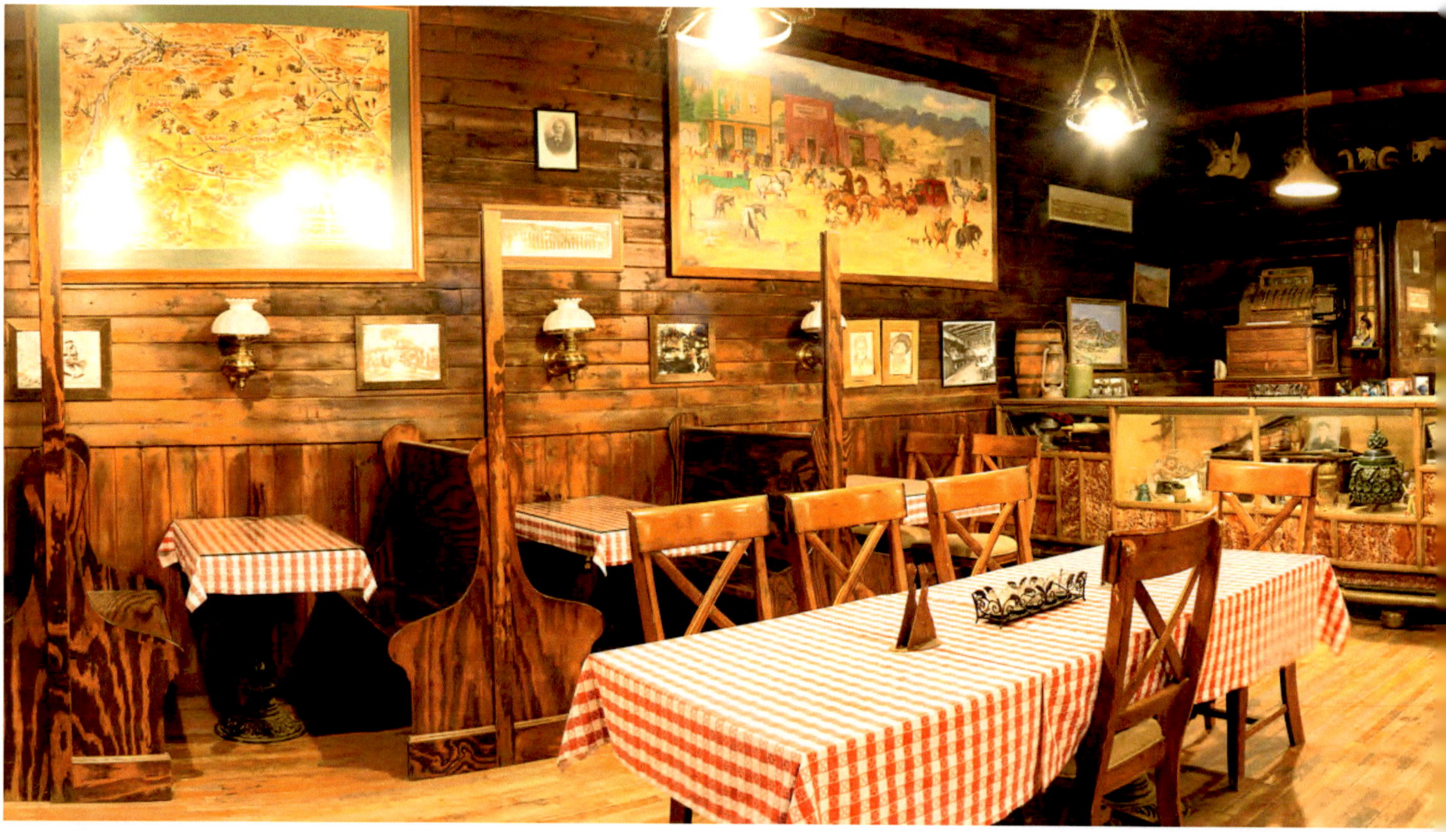

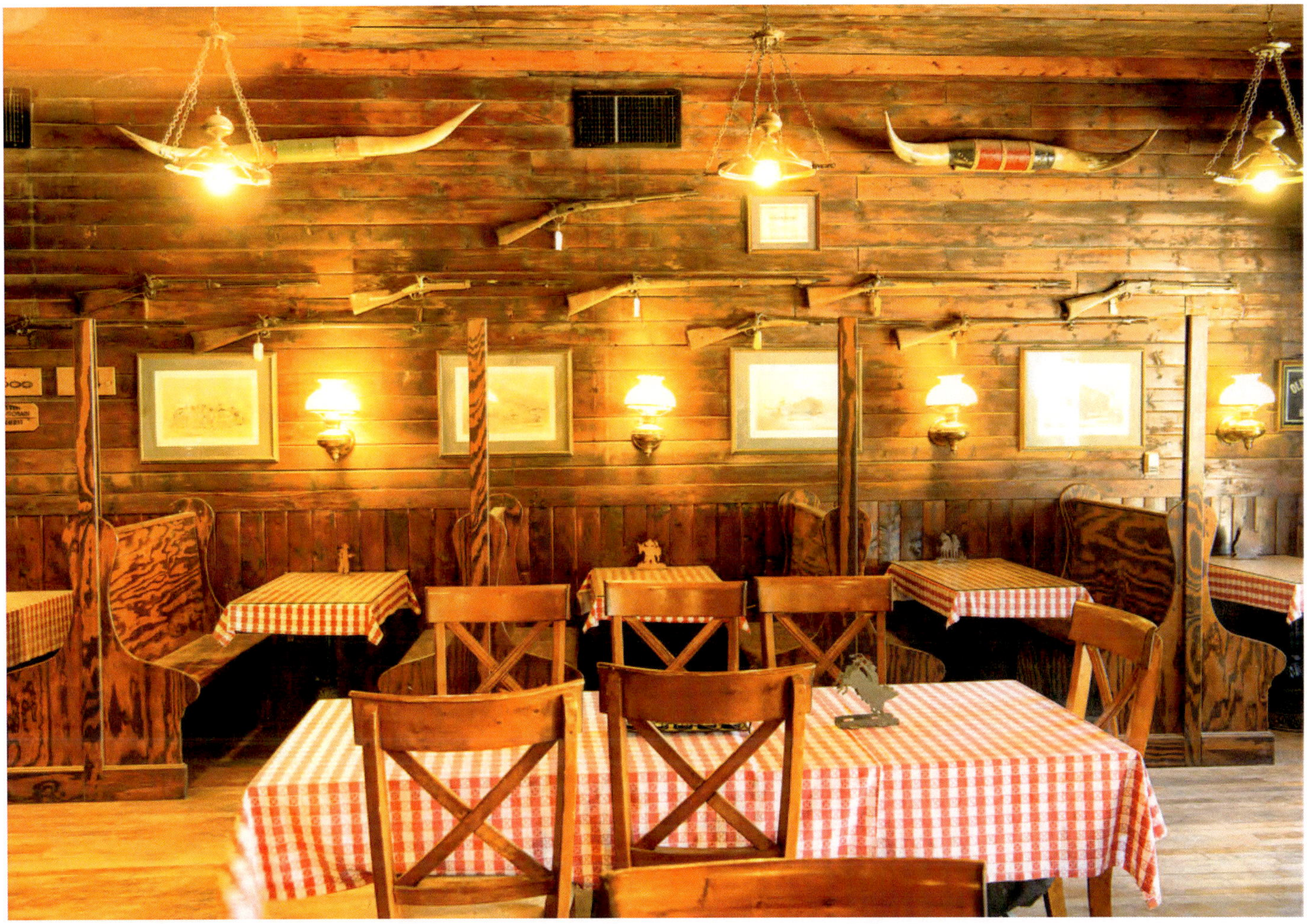

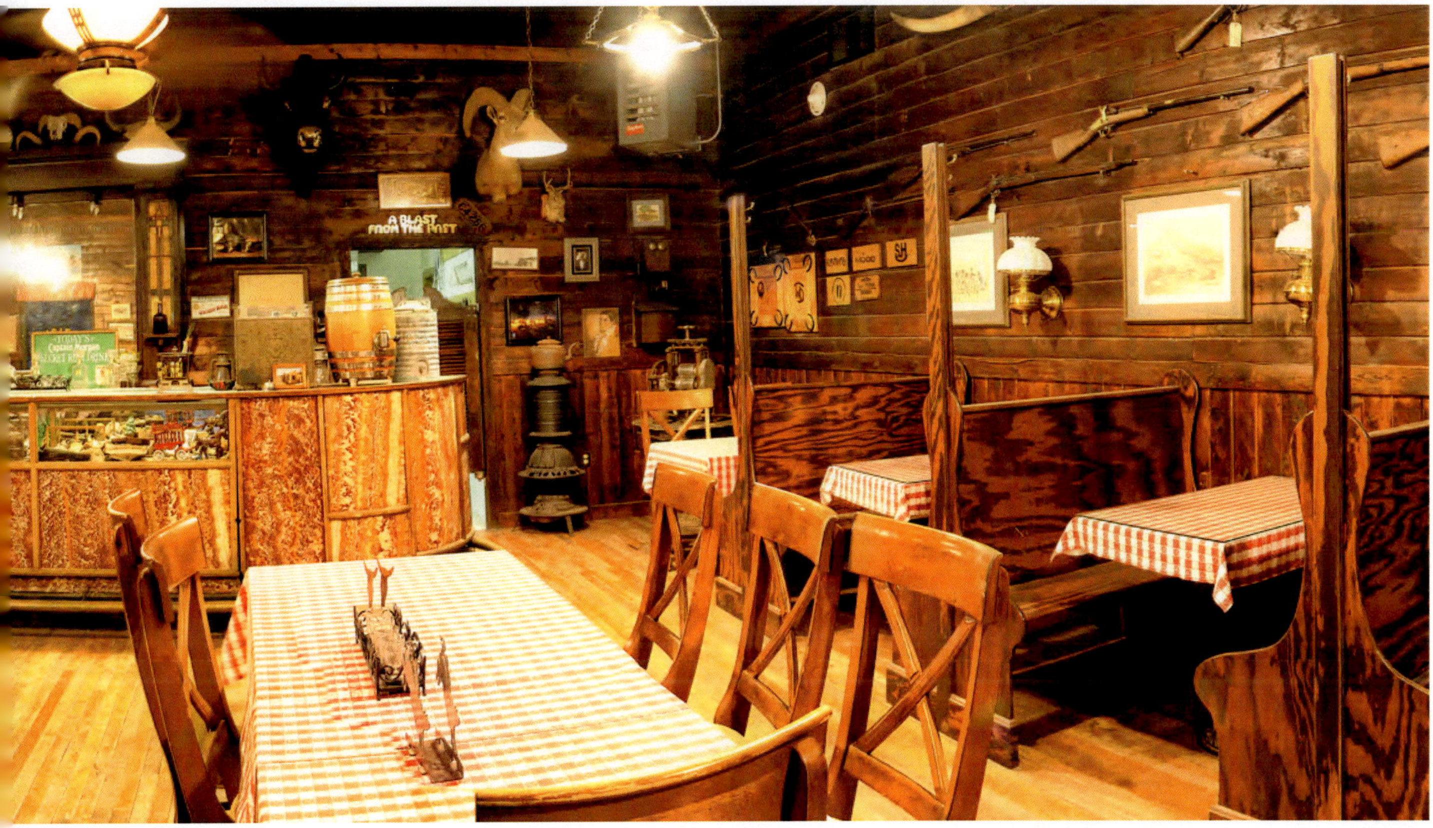

The Mercantile

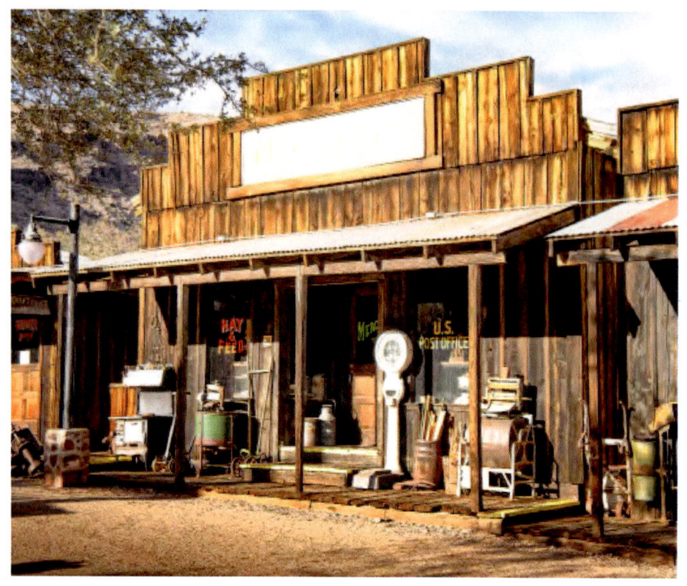

The Mercantile building was originally Dick Wick Hall's grocery store in Salone, Arizona. The Robsons purchased the building, dismantled the entire store, and reassembled it in its current spot. Now that they had a store, they needed to stock it. The items on the shelves are from a cache of unsold items found in storage for over 50 years from a store in Solomonville, Az

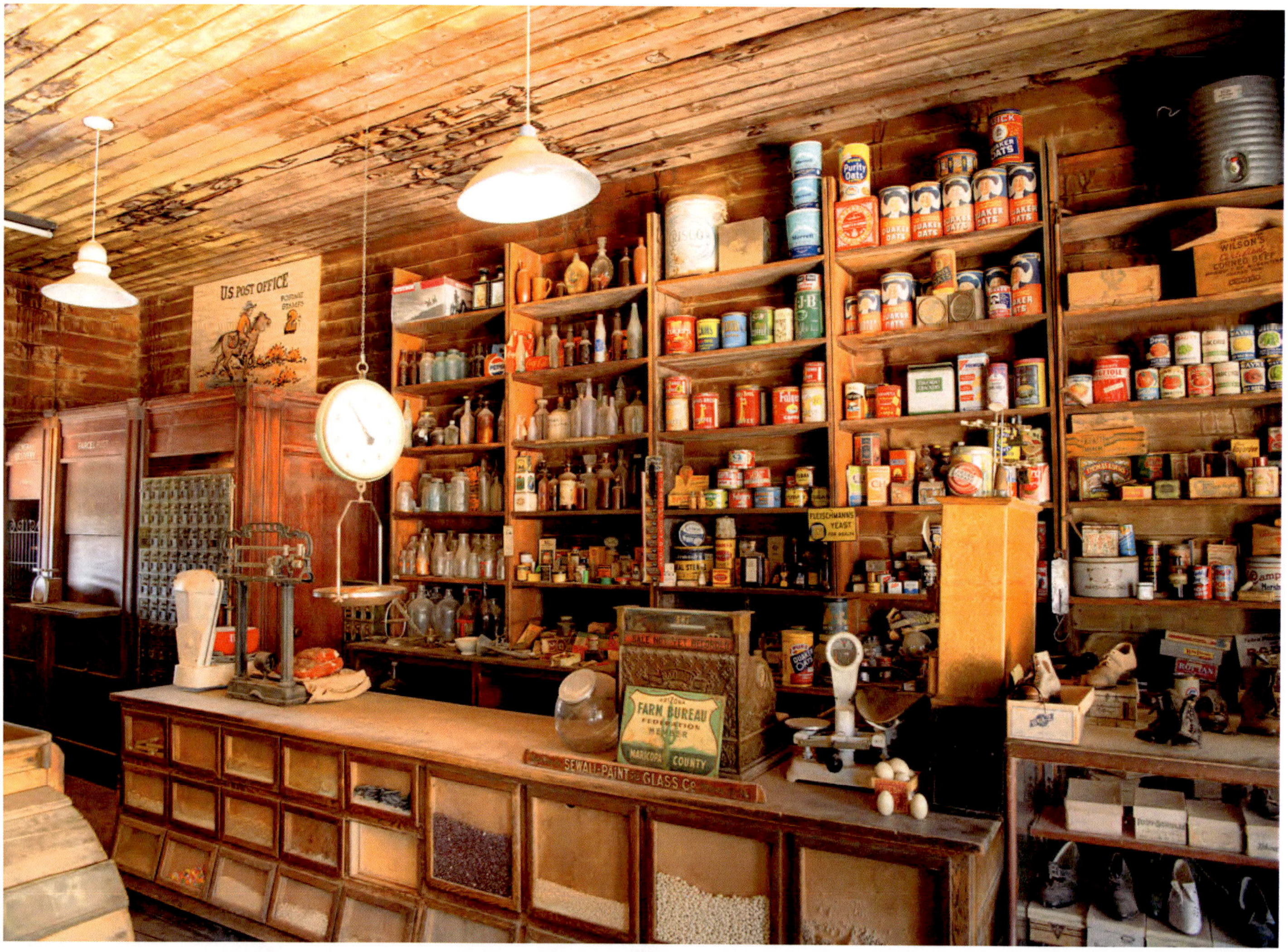

The Mercantile - Food and Spices

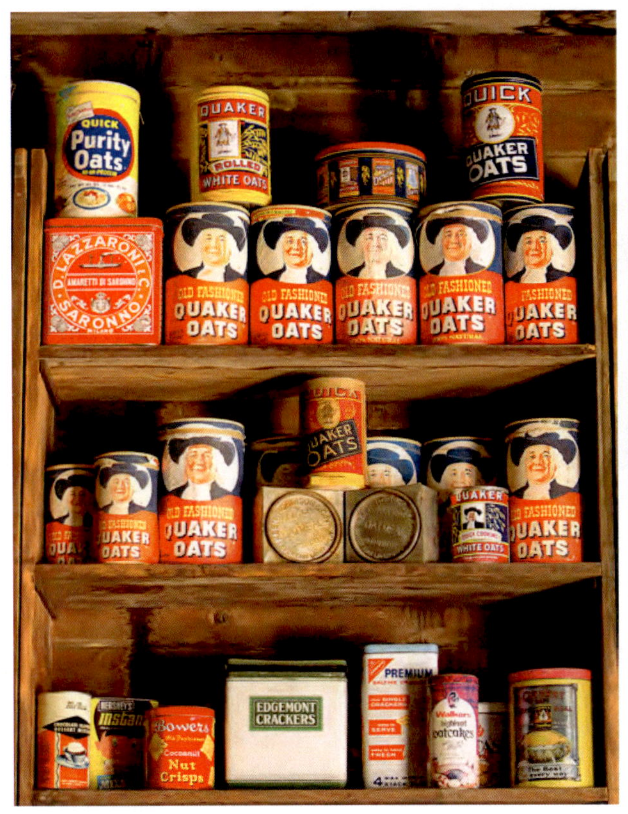

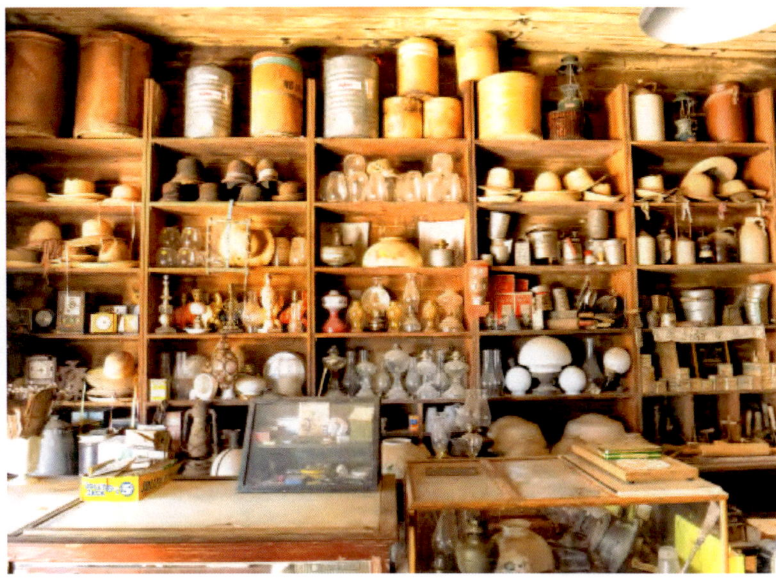

The Mercantile - Household Goods

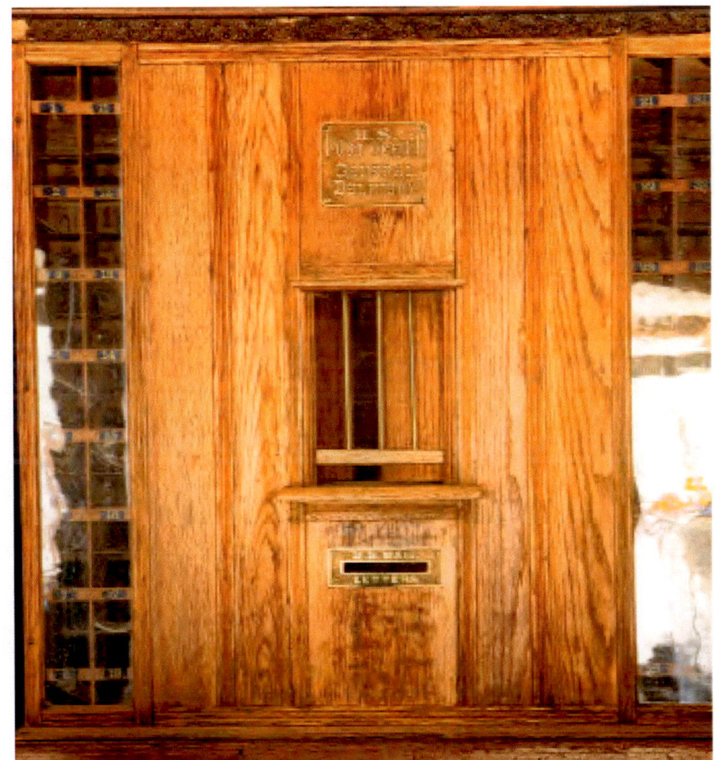

In the true nature of the early 1900s, general stores were the one-stop-shop of the town; not only could you buy whatever you needed, they routinely housed the town's post office.   In this spirit, the back of the store is set up as a Post Office.

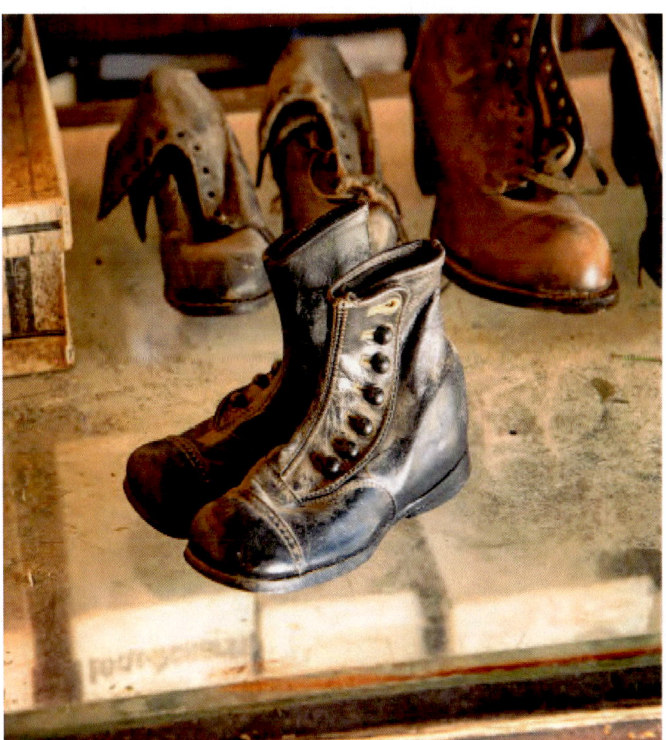

Vintage High Button Boots

Barbershop

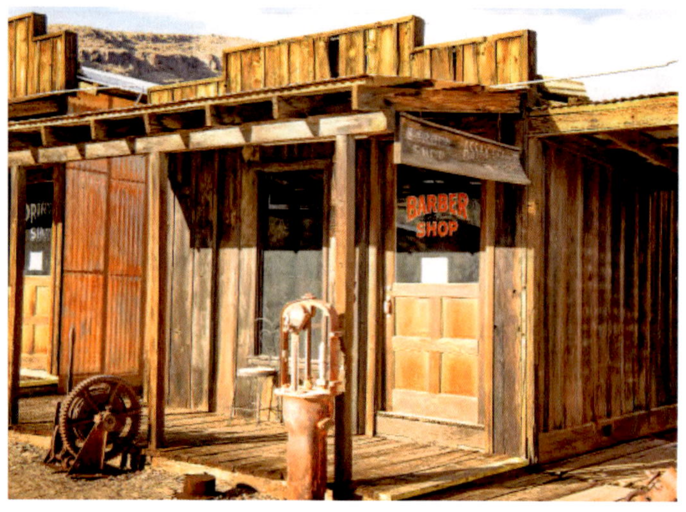 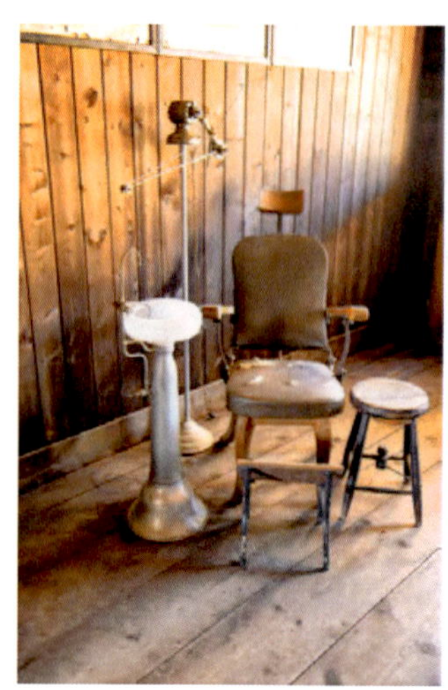

Standing in the barbershop, you feel like you have stepped into an old-time western movie. Many of the old west barbers also provided dental/medical services. Beyond the barber chairs, you see barber clippers, razors, tonics, and dental instruments.

No respective old west barbershop would be complete without a bath, which is represented here.

This dental chair and drill are on display in the barbershop. This dental chair and drill are on display in the barbershop.

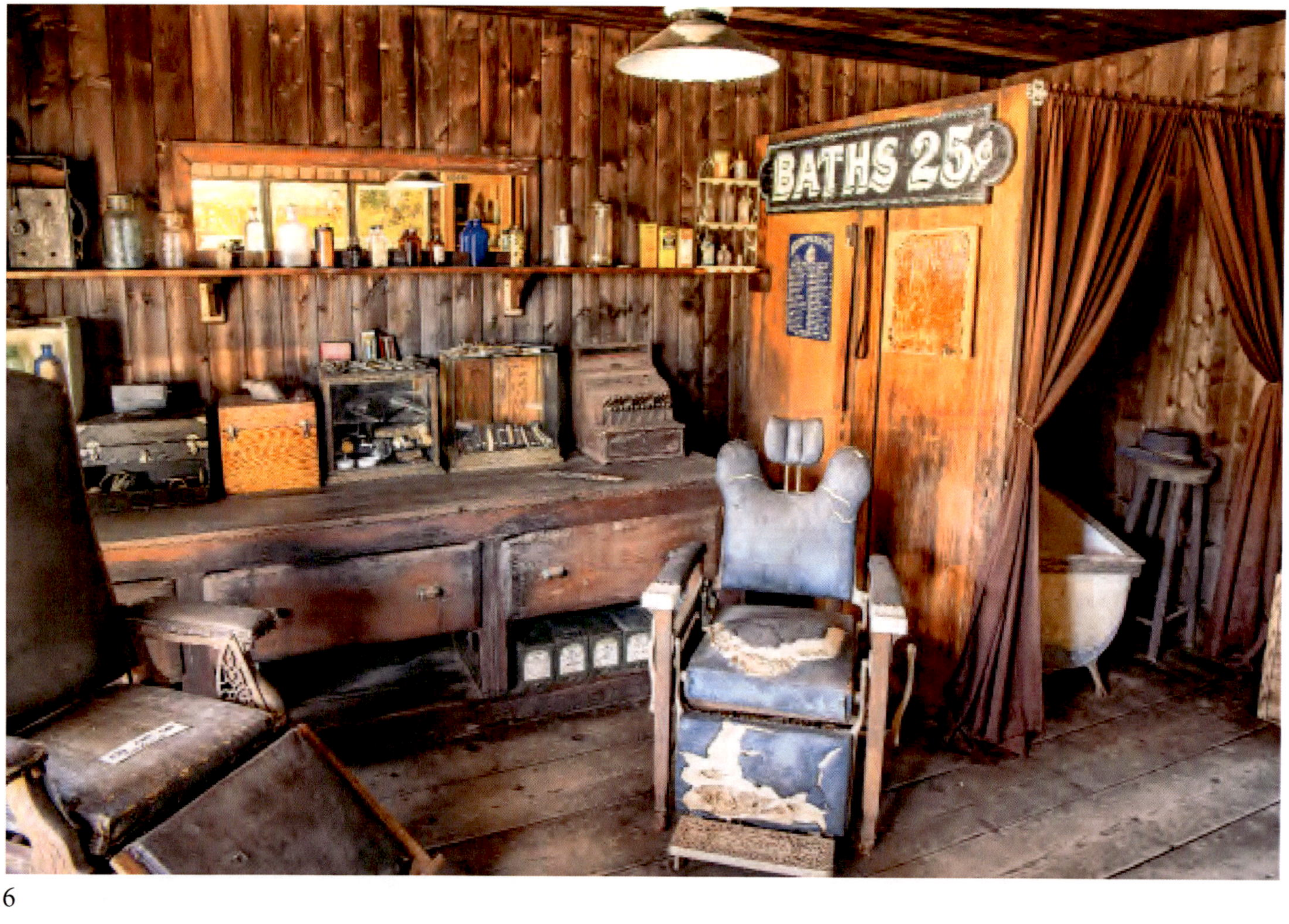

Assay Office

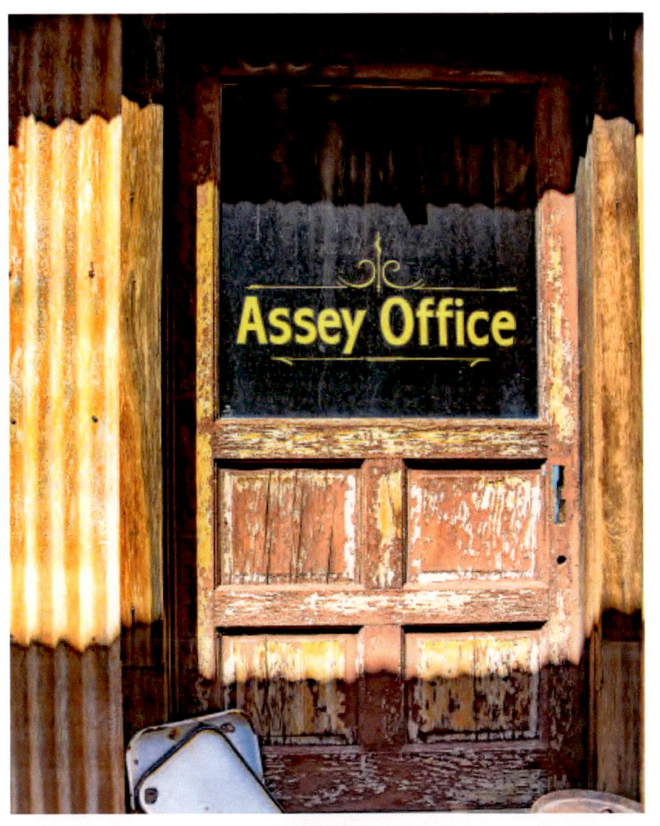

A mine assay office is a laboratory where samples of ore or mineral specimens are analyzed to determine the material's metal content and other properties. Assaying is the process of testing ore or minerals to determine their composition and quality. Mine assay offices are commonly found at mines and mineral processing facilities. The results of the assays performed at a mine assay office are used to guide the ore mining and processing and evaluate the material's economic value.

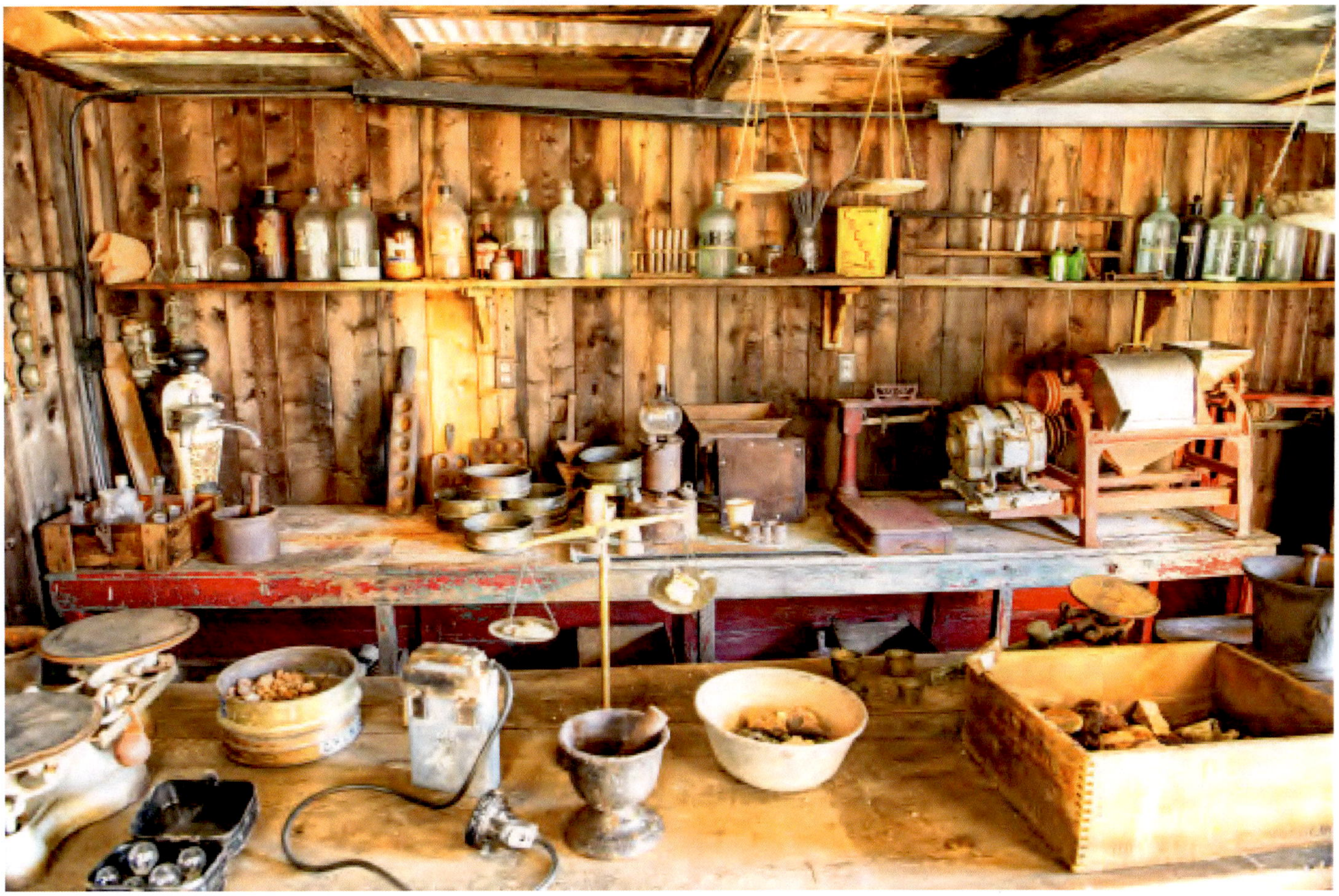

The Hillside Press

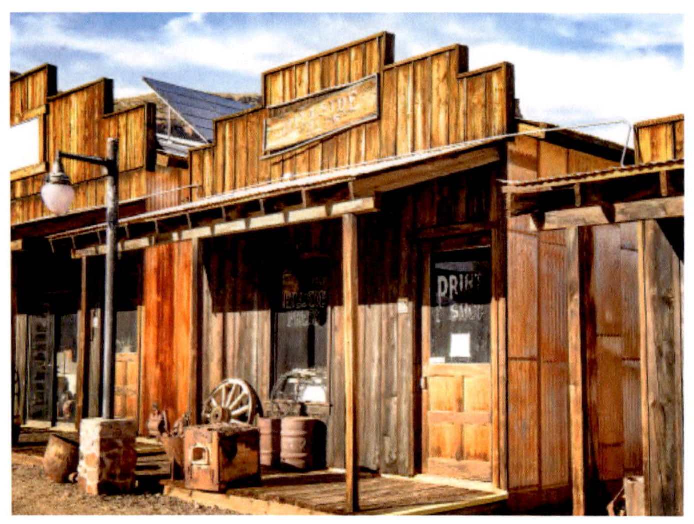

The Hillside Press is an old newspaper office. The press building has an antique linotype machine and a typewriter collection that would make Tom Hanks proud.

Generating Plant

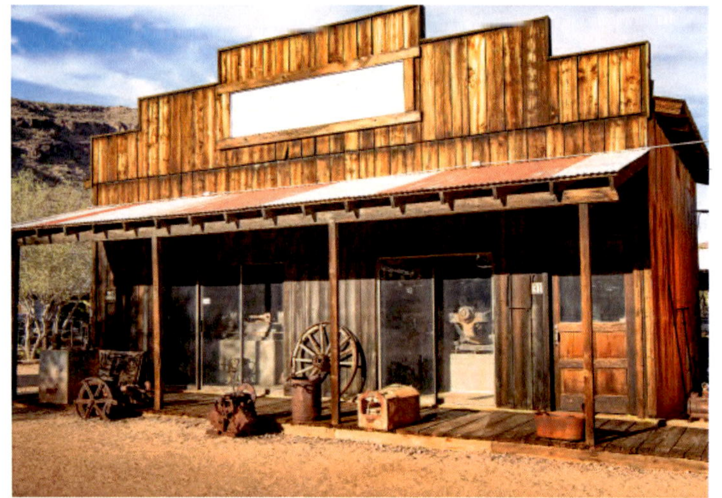

Early western towns were responsible for generating their power. The Generating Plant building represents this fact; in this case, inside the building is a huge steam-powered generator. This generator once provided power to the town of Kingman, Arizona.

One of the reasons this town gives us the feeling of the old west is that you do not see any utility lines.

Just like in the old days, Robson's Arizona Mining World is responsible for its own power. Instead of steam power, it relies on solar power. Behind the large steam generator, you will see the bank of solar batteries to store the energy provided by the panels on the roof. Here the old meets the new.

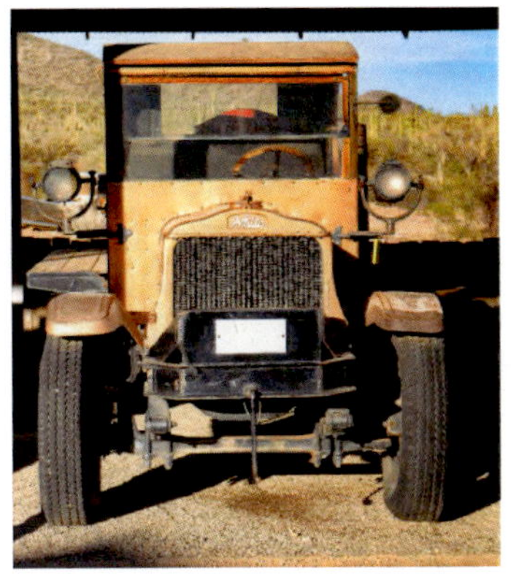

1919 White Truck

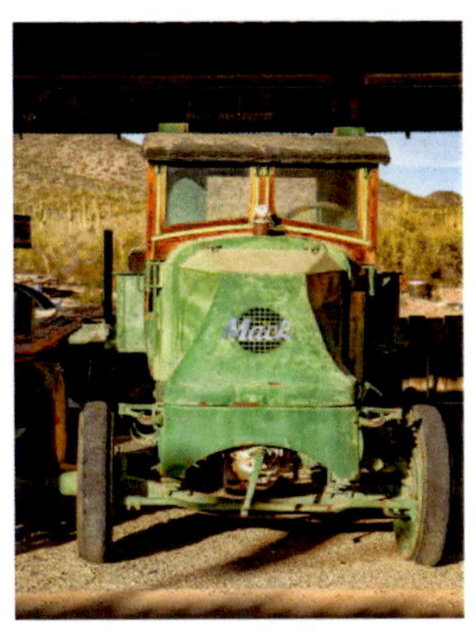

1912 Mack Truck

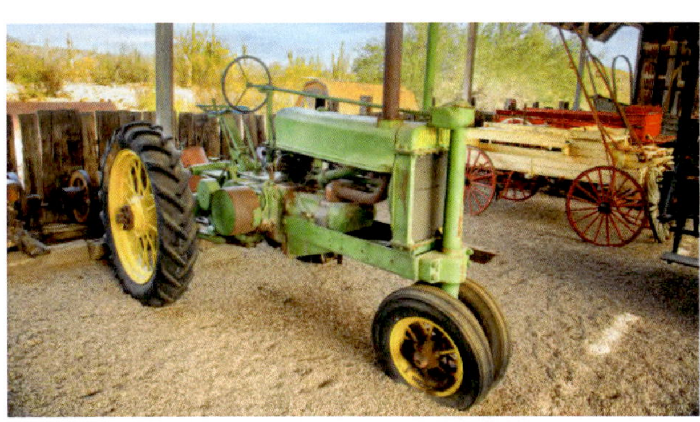

1948 Unstlyed B John Deere

Behind main street, you will find the Carriage House. the Carriage hours has an assortment of old cars, trucks, wagons, utility engines, and farm tractors. Here is a sample of what you will find.

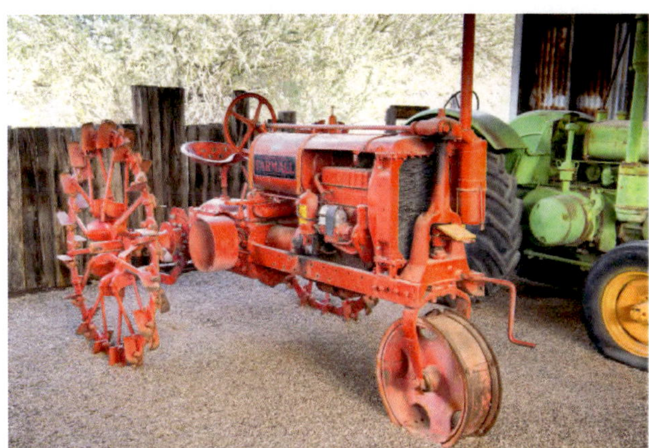

1928 Farmall on Steel Wheels

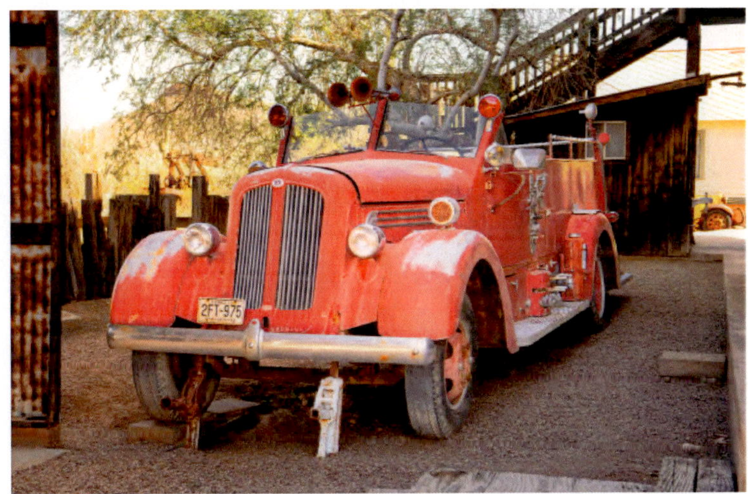

1941 Seagraves Fire Engine

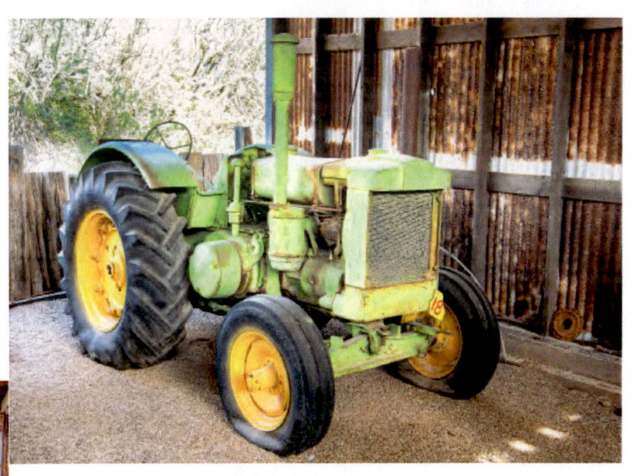

1932 John Deere GP

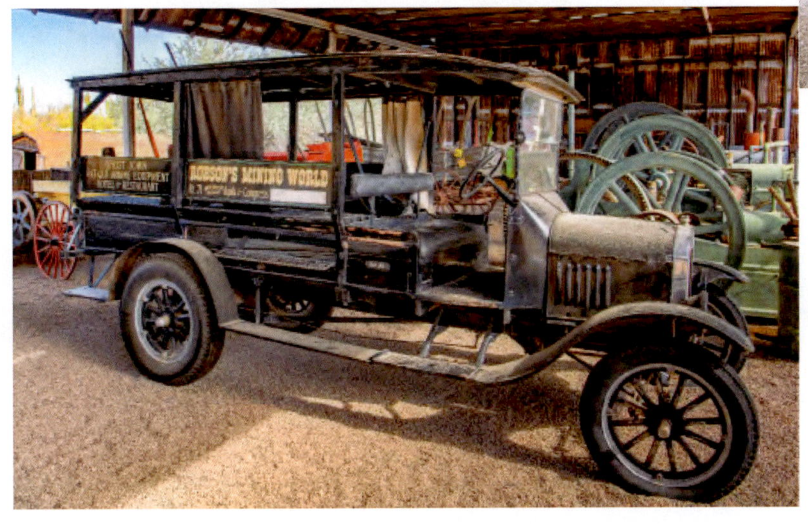

Model T 1926 Ford Delivery Wagon

The Southside of Main Street

The south side of Main Street is home to Charles's extensive collection of mining equipment. This is a sample of some of the items on display.

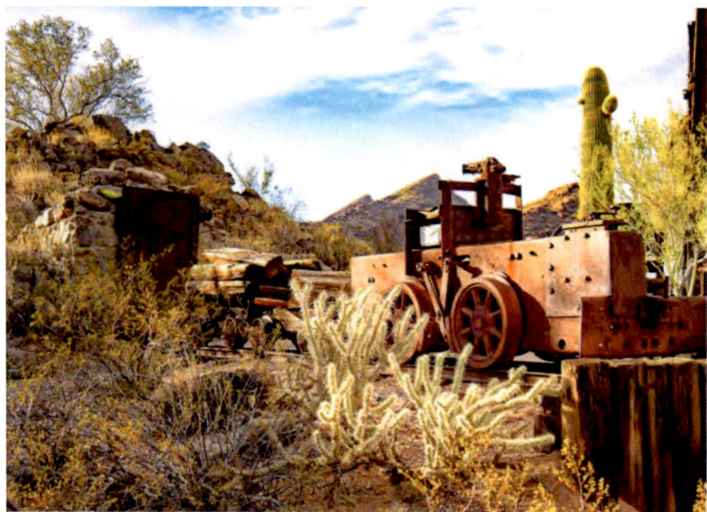

1900's Manche - Electric Ore Car Mover

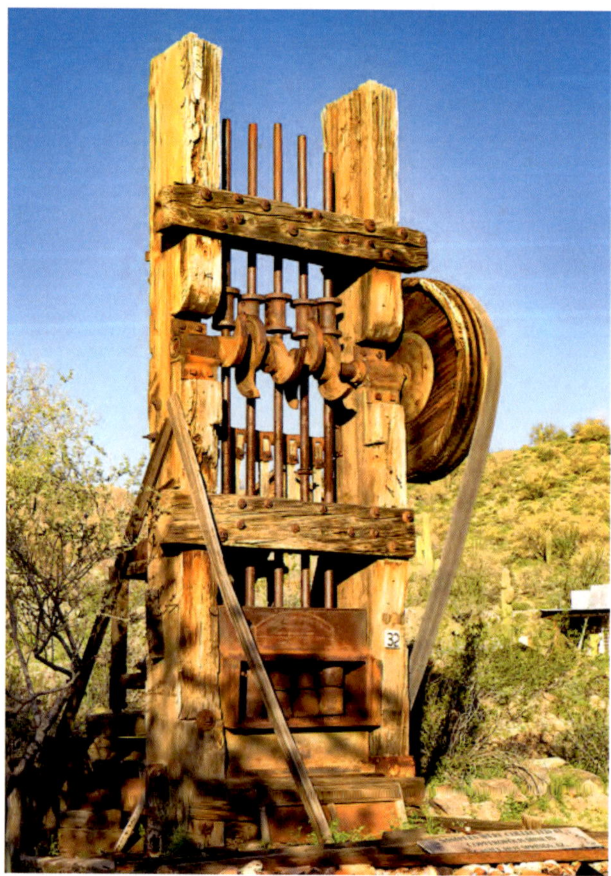

5 Hammer Stamp Mill

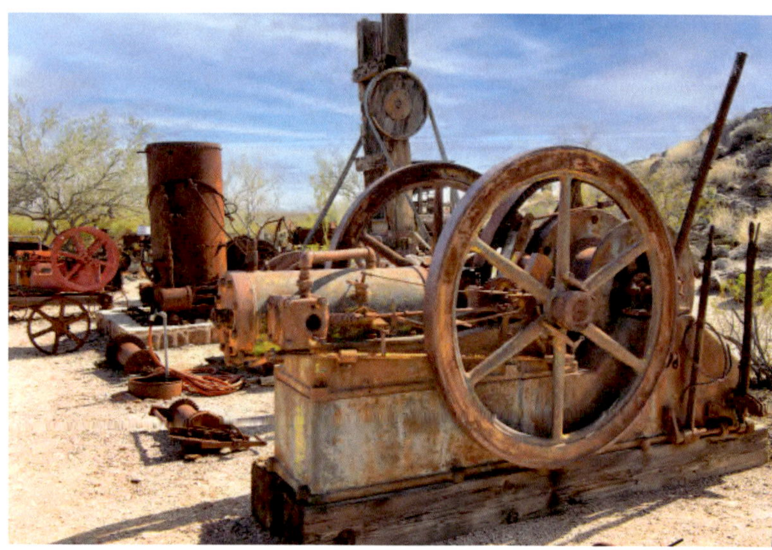

Large Air Compressor

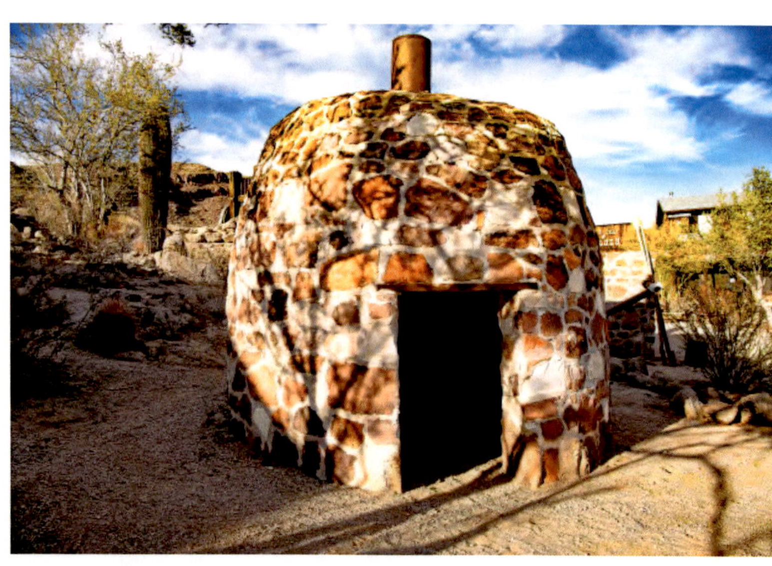

Beehive Charcoal Furnace - Supported Smelting

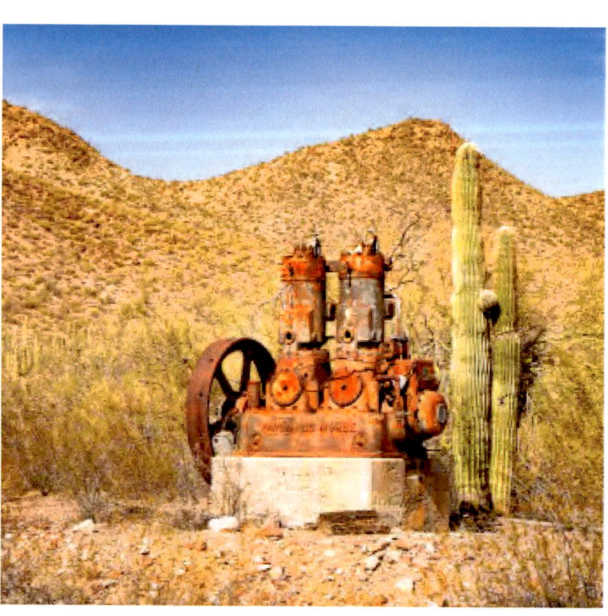

Fairbanks-Morse Engine

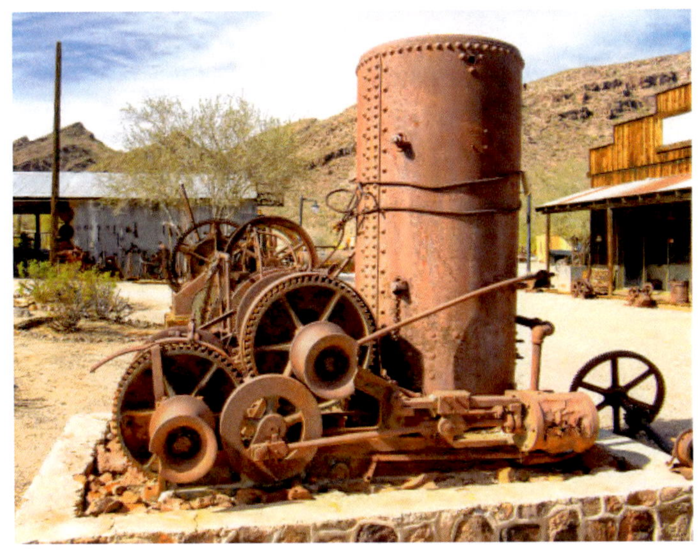

Steam Hoist - Lifted Equipment into and out of the Mine

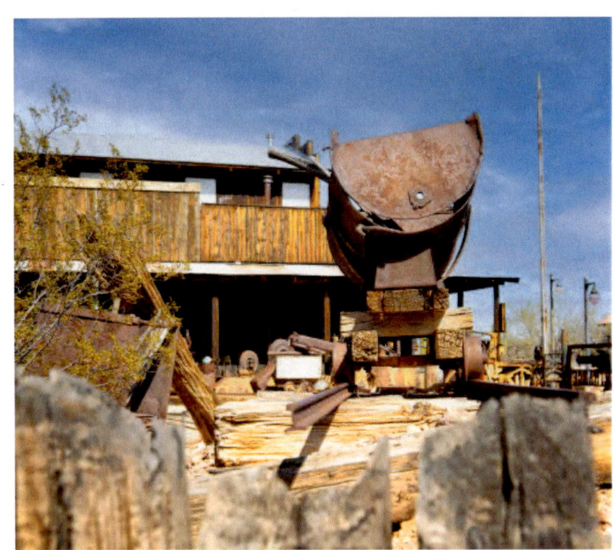

Ore Car On Track

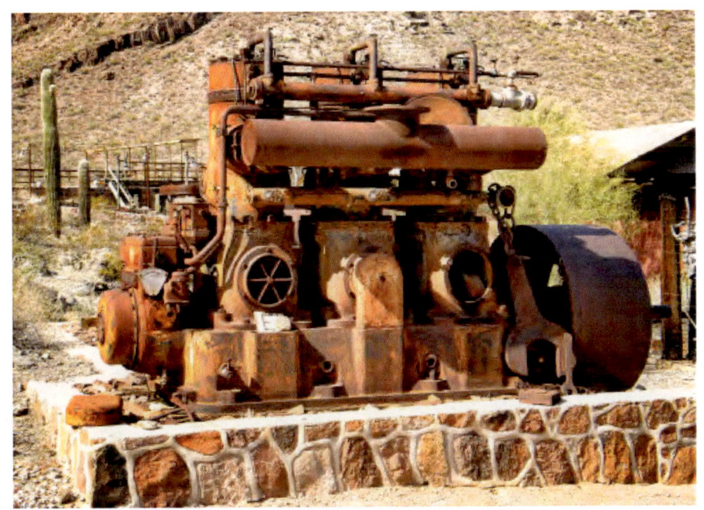

Old Engine

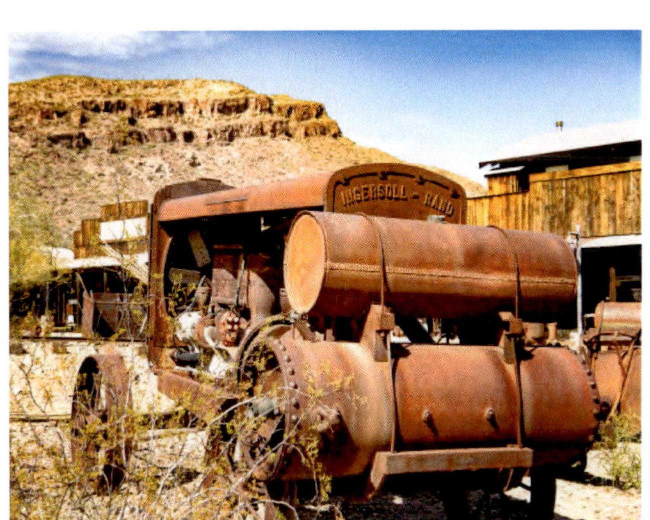

Ingersoll-Rand Compressor

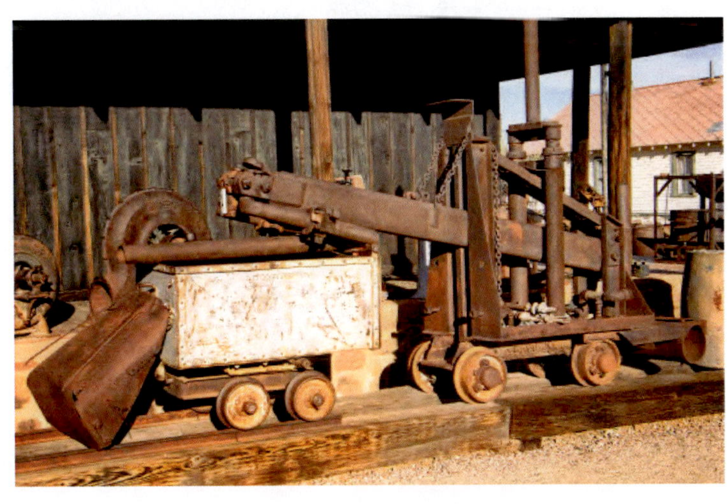

Jumbo - Air Driven Drill Rig

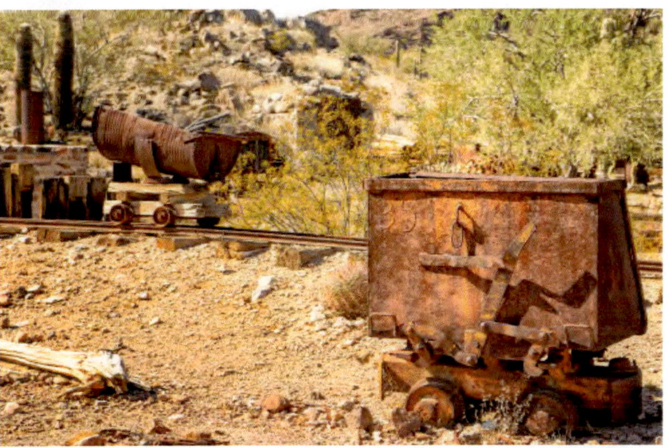

Ore Car

Blacksmith/Machine Shop

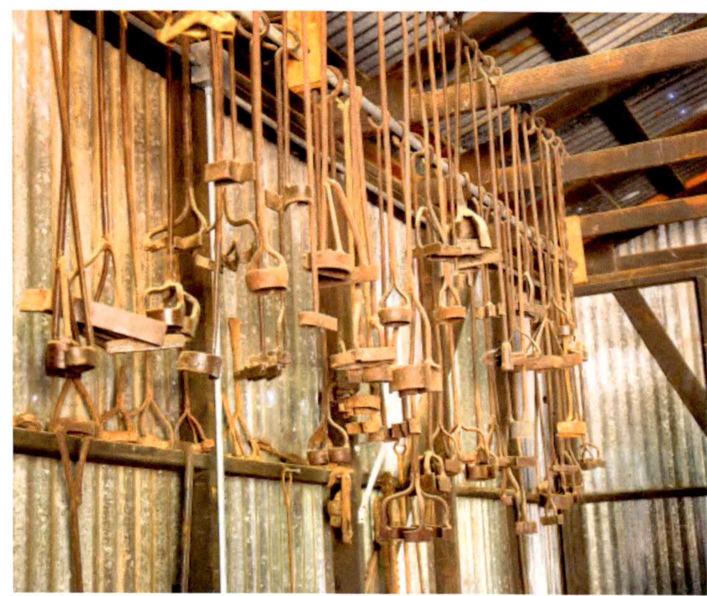

Large Collection of Branding Irons

Strolling west from the mining equipment displays, you come to the blacksmith and machine shops. These shops were critical to mining operations. The centerpiece of the blacksmith shop is the forge, and this is where metal is heated and shaped into whatever is needed to keep the mine operations running. Besides all of the tools of the trade, there is also an extensive collection of branding irons.

The machine shop (Right) also supports the mine by turning out replacement parts needed to keep the mining machines humming. This machine shop is set up as most shops were in the early 1900s, unlike today, where we are accustomed to all equipment having its own electric motor to provide power. Early shops had a single engine (steam, gas, or electric) that provided power to tools via a belt and pulley system.

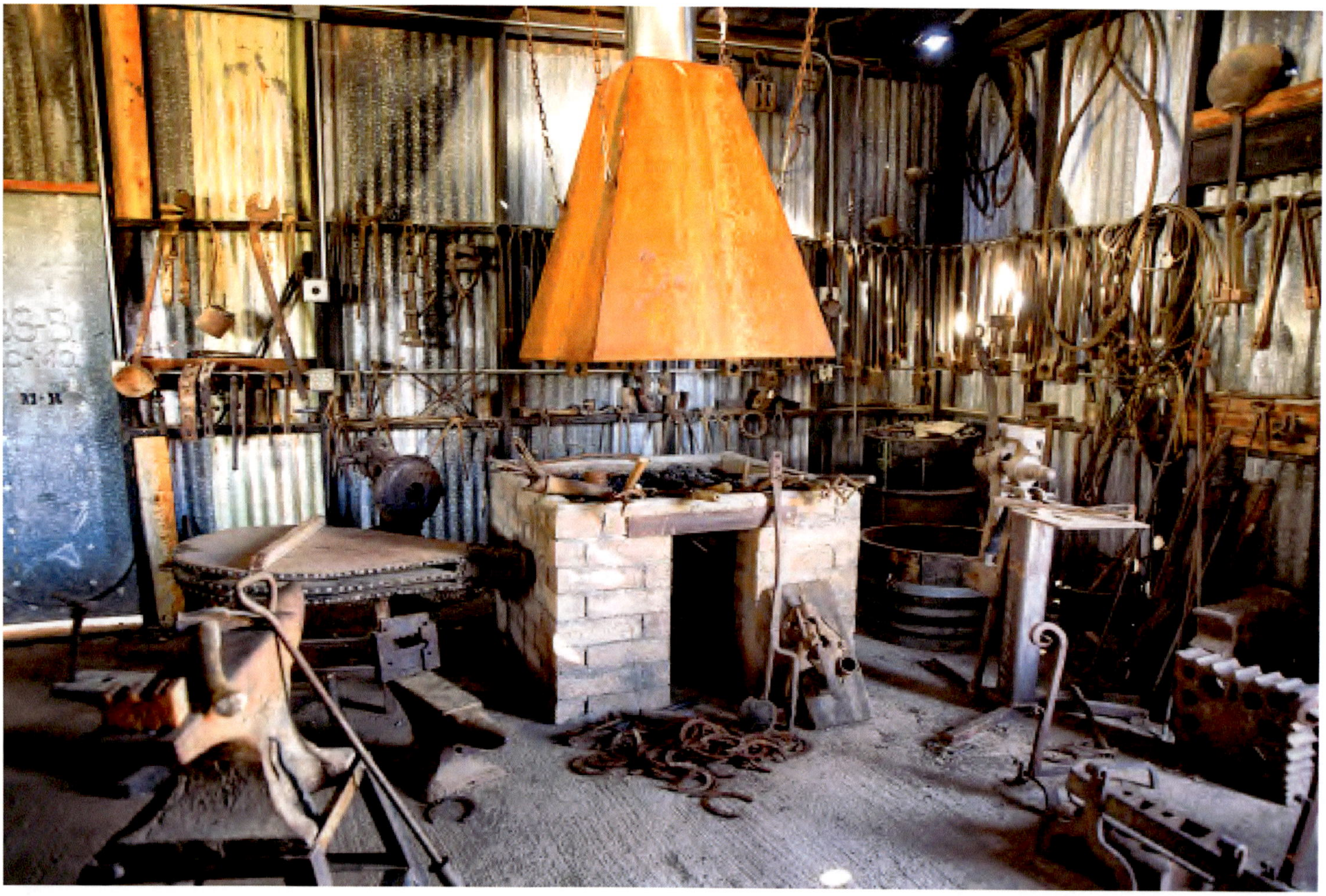

Black Smith Forge

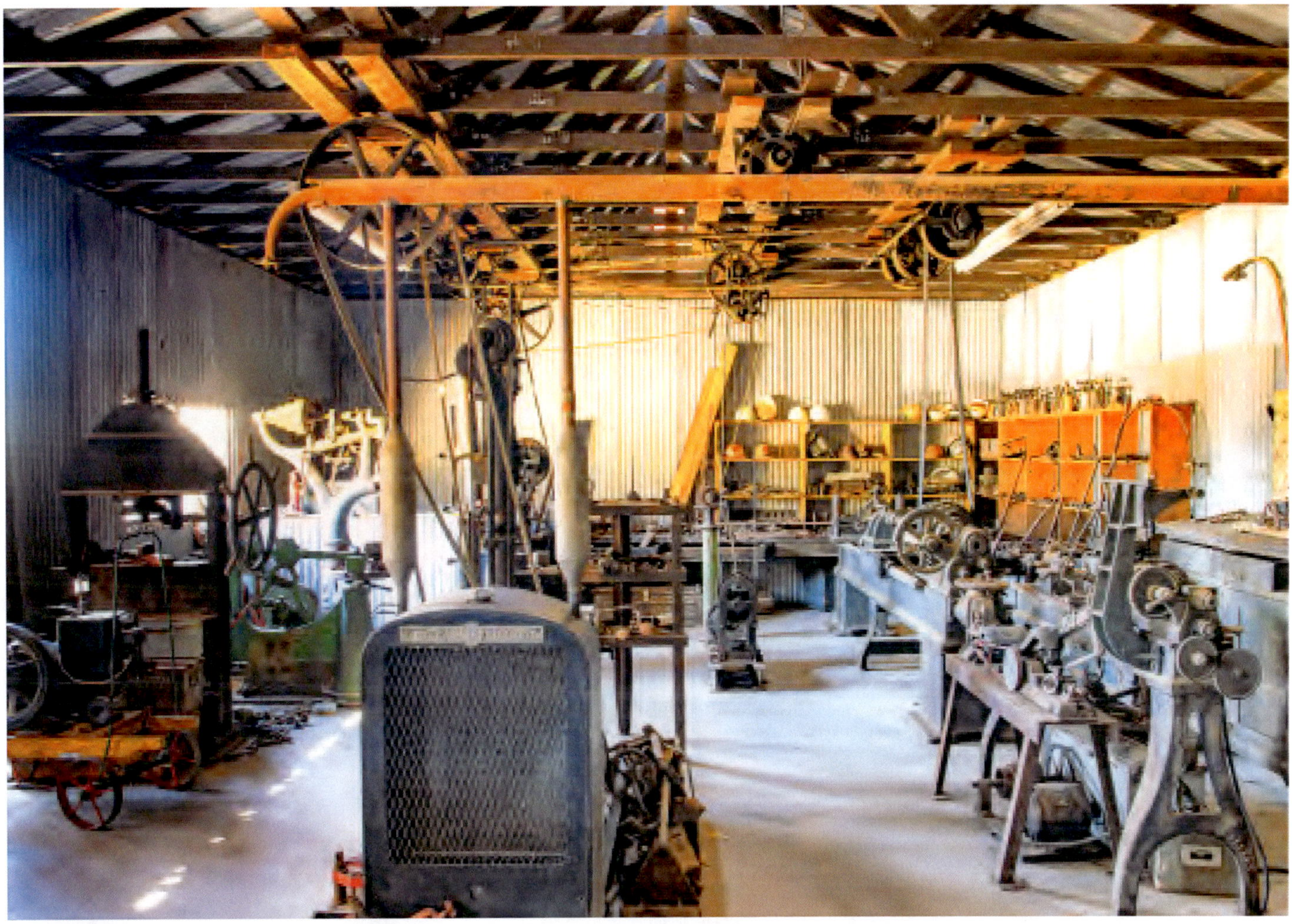

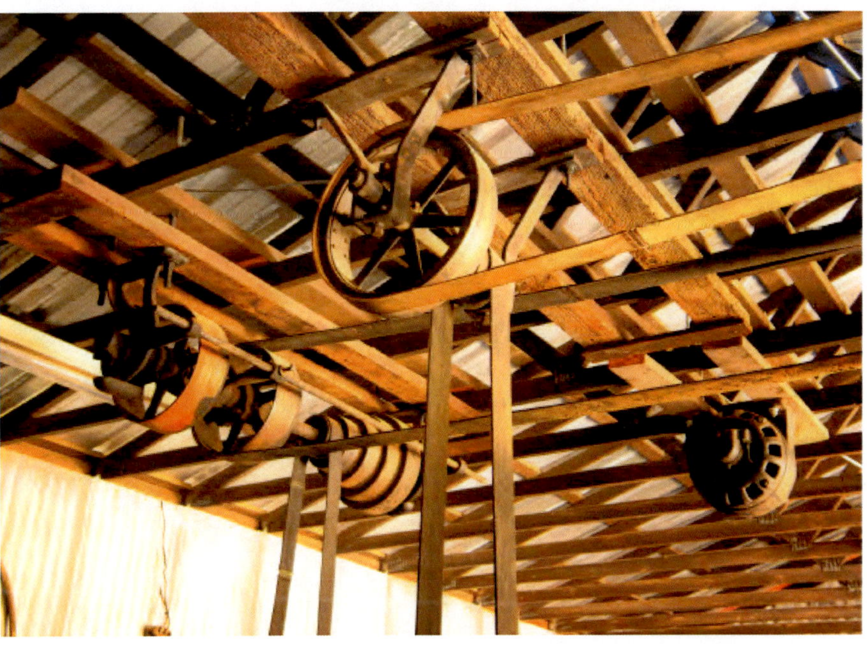

Machine Shop

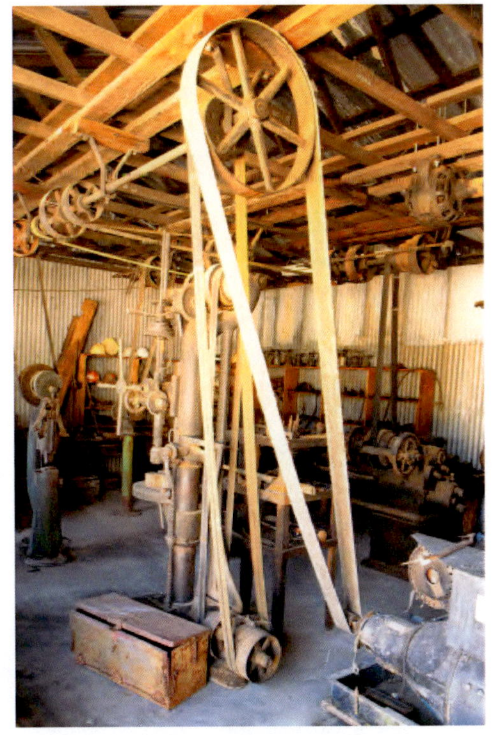

Main Shop Motor

Belt Line

Around Town

Walking the town and the surrounding area, you can find treasures around every corner.

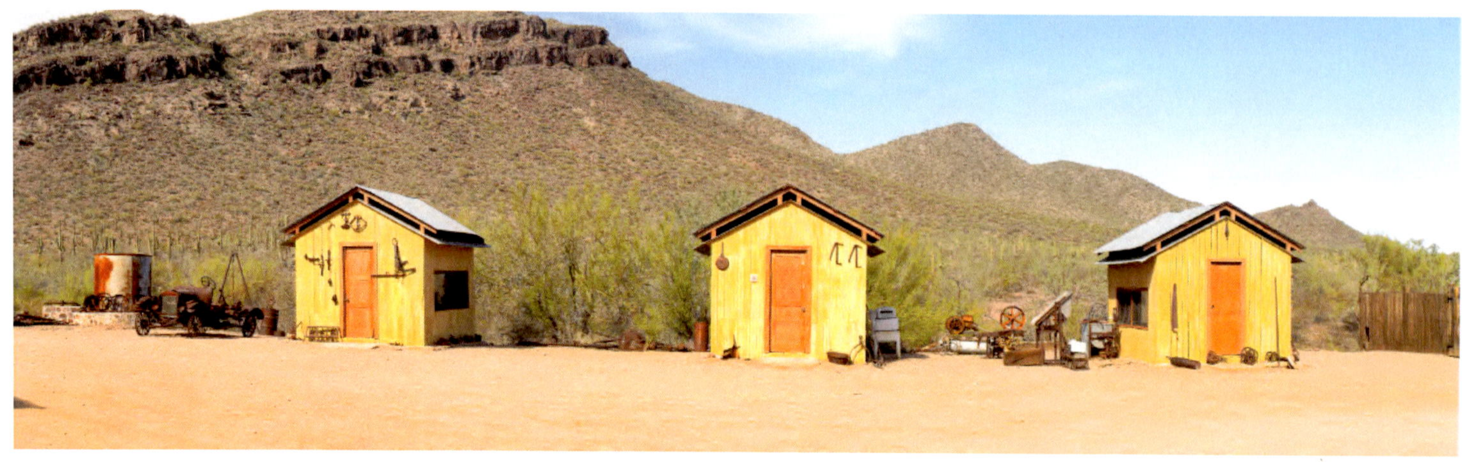

Three Miners Cabins

These Miners' cabins provided housing for the miners over the years. To help deal with the extreme Sonoran Desert heat, these cabins were built with two roofs with an air gap.

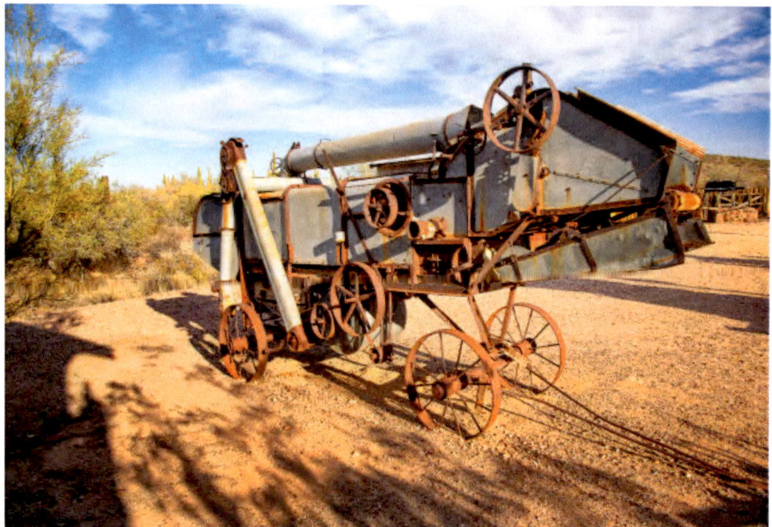

J.I. Case Threshing Machine

While this is not a piece of mining equipment, as with the tractors on display in the carriage house, the Robsons recognized the importance of Arizona's farming industry.

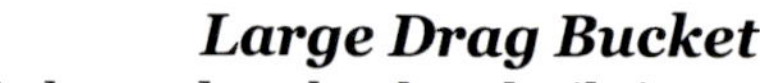

Large Drag Bucket

This large drag bucket, built in 1958, was the largest in the world at the time of its manufacture.

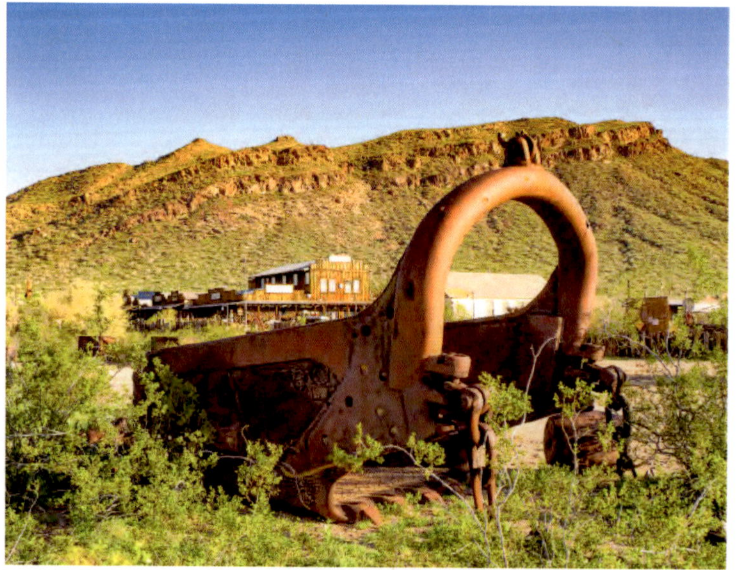

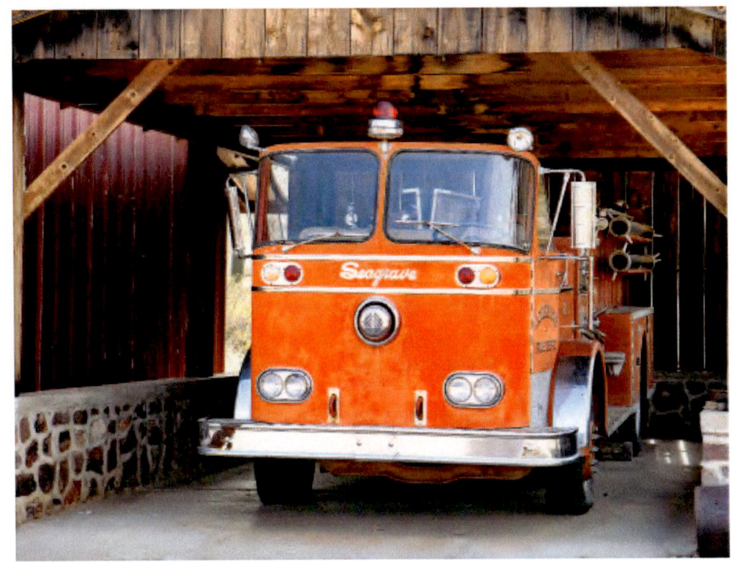

1968 Seagrave Fire Engine

The Fire Engine seems poised to roll out if needed. This engine proudly served the city of Wickenberg, Arizona.

If this engine looks familiar, that may be because this is the same model of fire truck that was the model for the fire truck in the Pixar movie Cars.

Large Headframe Pulley

We found this headframe pulley in the desert between the town and the surrounding hills.

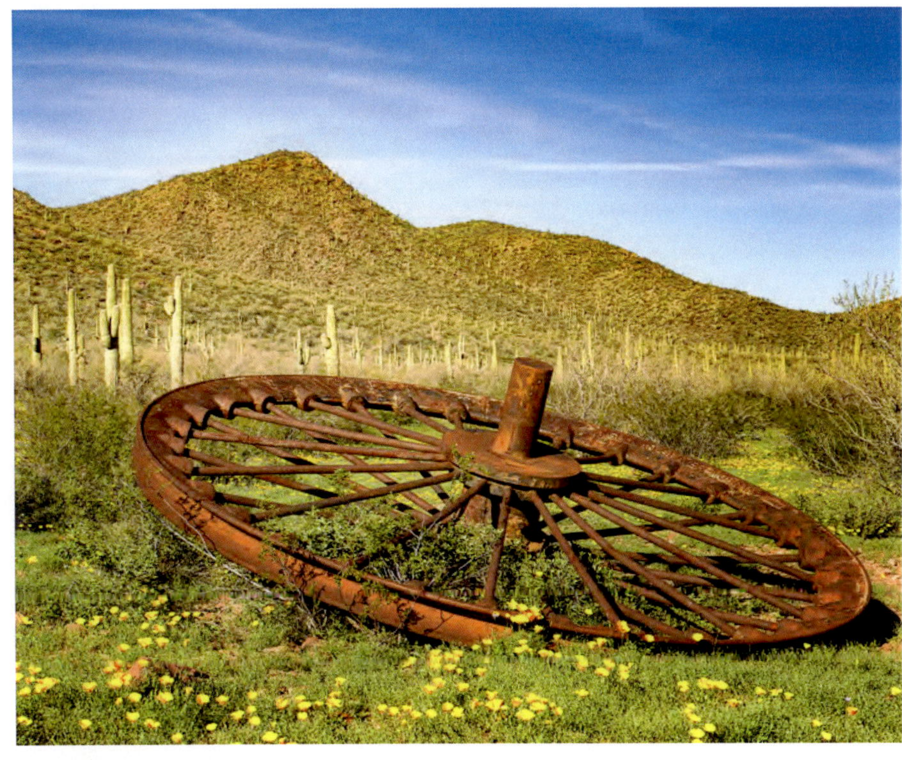

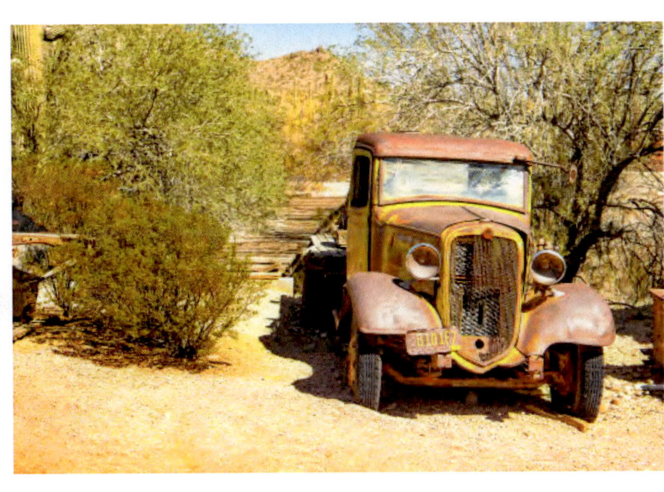

Old General Motors Truck

The Chapel

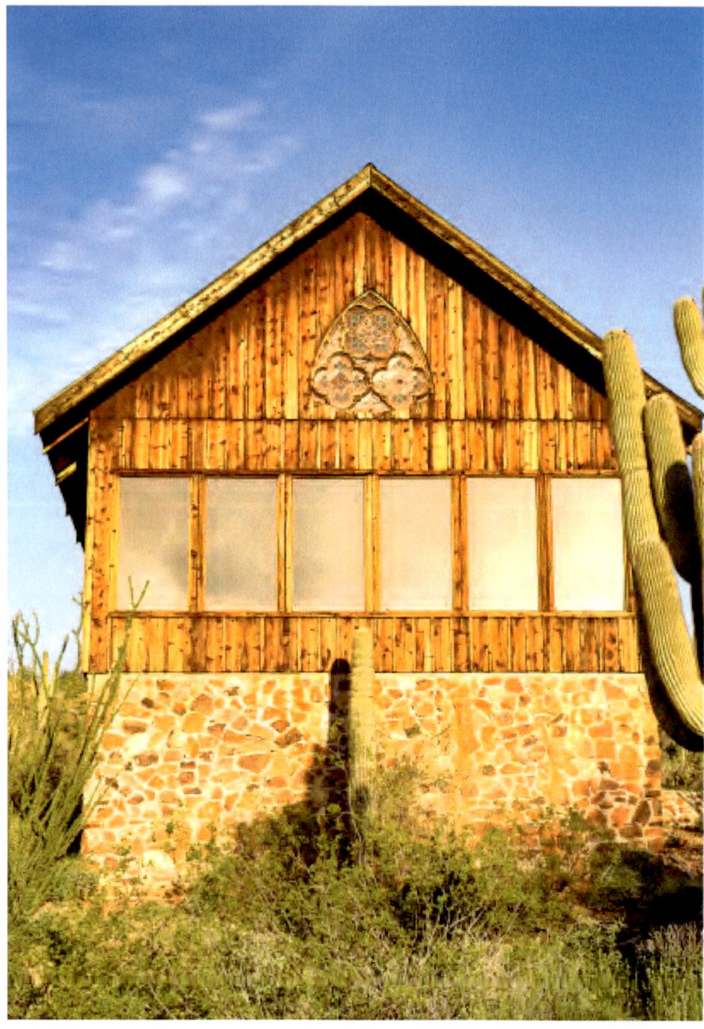

The Chapel is built on a hill behind the fire engine house

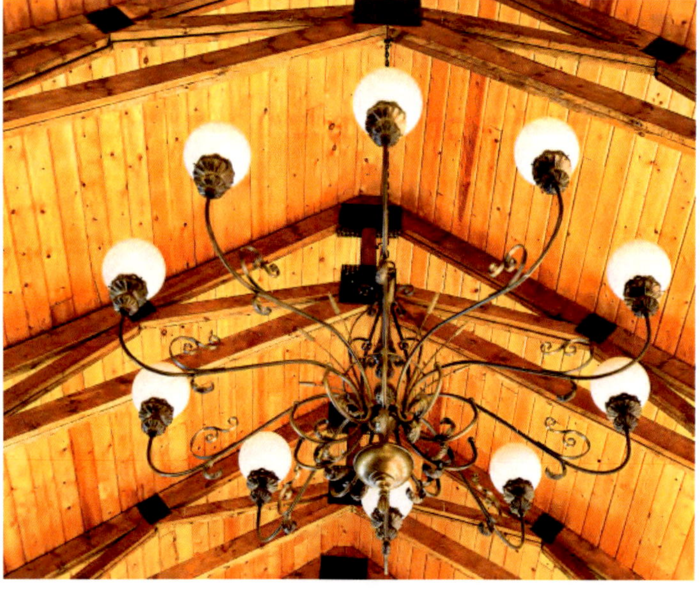

Antique Chandelier

The Robsons obtained many of the items in their collection by attending auctions. In some cases, they would buy the entire lot to ensure they could get the item they were interested in. This is how the Chapel became part of the town. Returning from an auction, Jeri Robson presented Charles with two large stained glass windows and convinced him to build the Chapel.

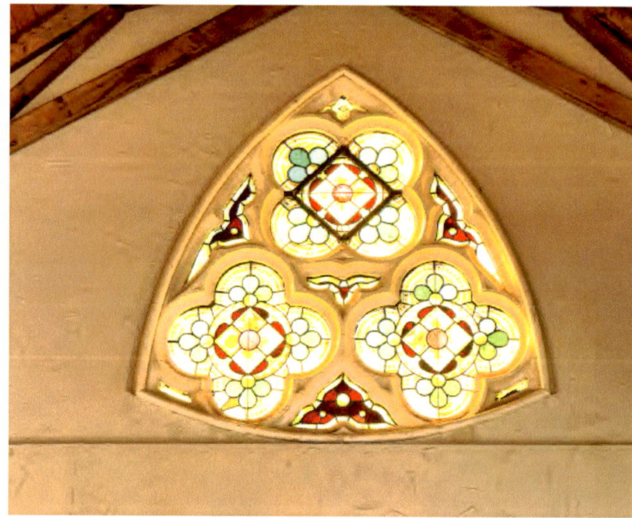

One half of the pair of stained glass windows.

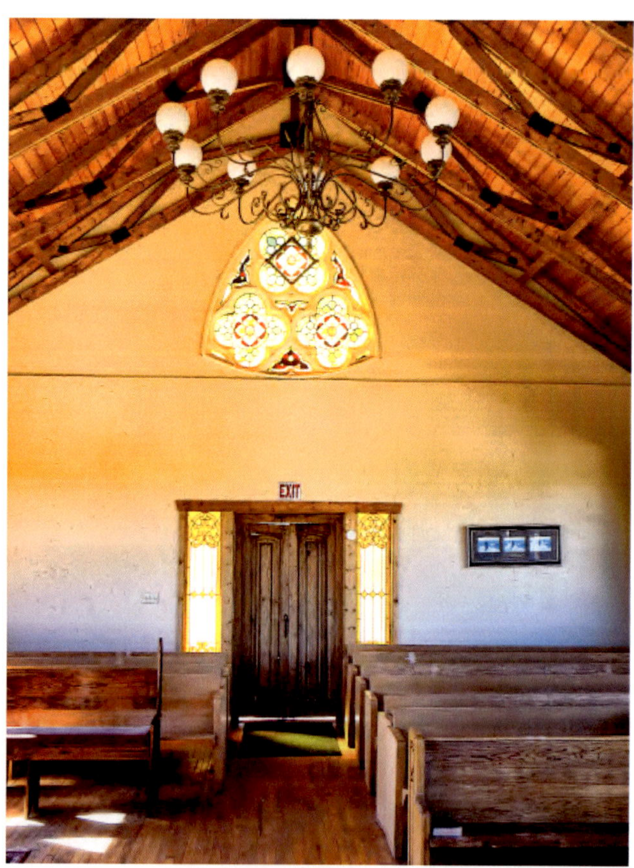

Chapel Interior

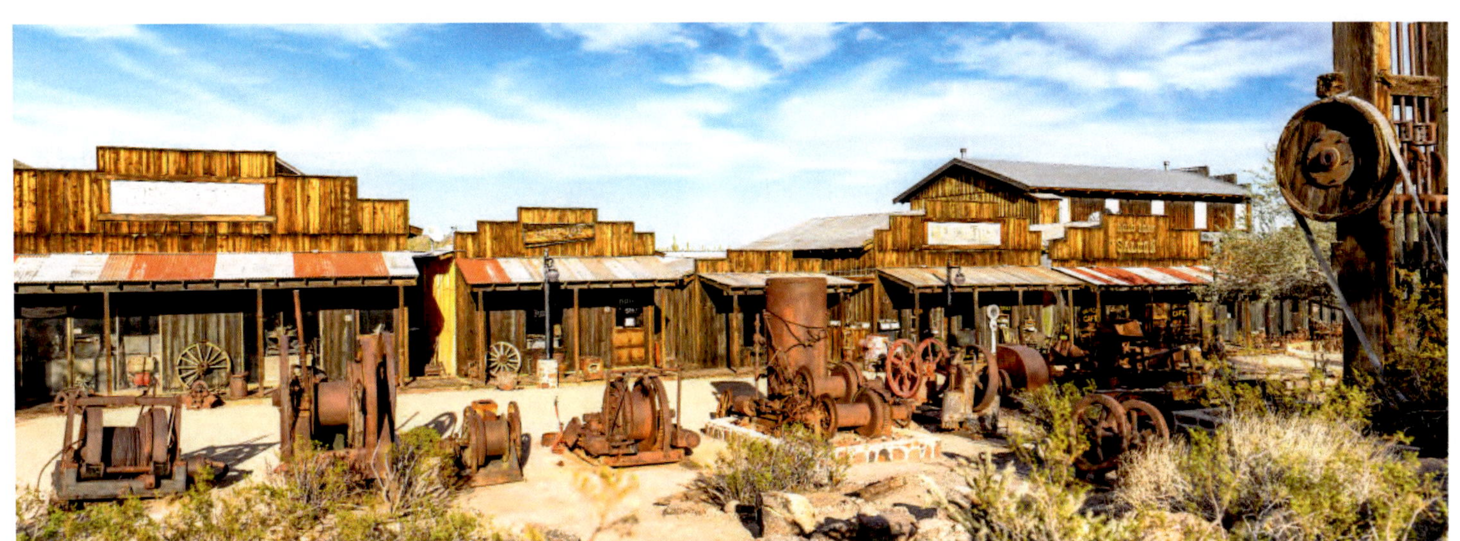

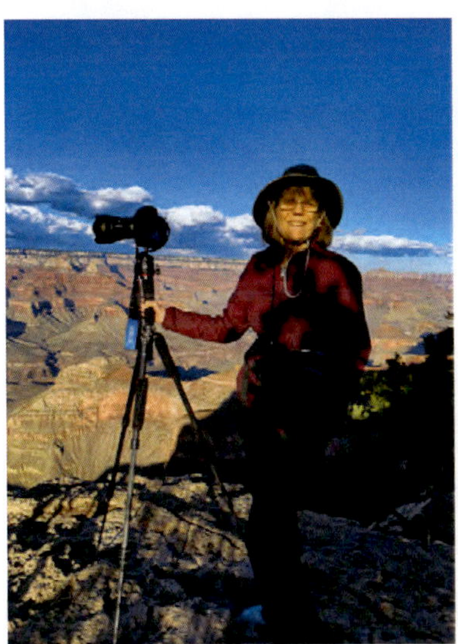

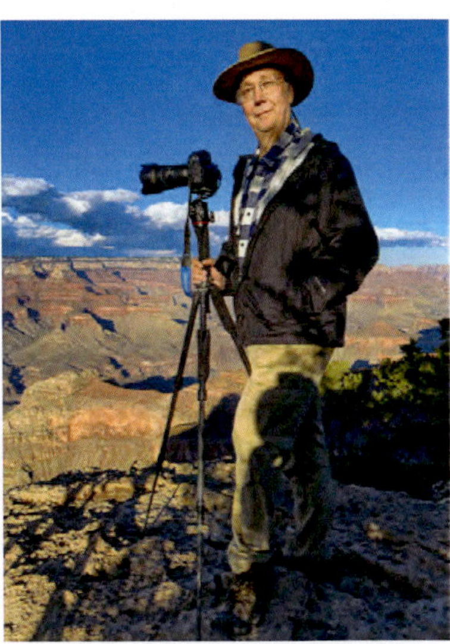

Fine Art Photographers Teresa and Keith Peters

Hello, we are Teresa and Keith Peters, also known as T&K Images. Our company was established in 1991, and throughout the years, we have cultivated a unique style that captures the stunning beauty and serenity of our world. Our main objective is to venture out and discover the ideal lighting to showcase the incredible planet we inhabit.

imagesbytk.com

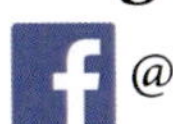 @T&K Images

 @ tkimagesfineartphotography